# EMUS CAN'T WALK
## BACKWARDS

# EMUS CAN'T
# WALK
# BACKWARDS

## ANOTHER ROUND OF
## DUBIOUS PUB FACTS

ROBERT ANWOOD

EBURY
PRESS

1 3 5 7 9 10 8 6 4 2

First published in 2007 by Ebury Press, an imprint of Ebury Publishing

A Random House Group Company

Text © Robert Anwood 2007
www.robertanwood.com

The Random House Group Limited Reg. No. 954009

Addresses for companies within the Random House Group can be found at
www.randomhouse.co.uk

A CIP catalogue record for this book is available from the British Library

Illustrator: Sarah Nayler
Design: Nicky Barneby and Tony Lyons

The Random House Group Limited makes every effort to ensure that
the papers used in our books are made from trees that have been legally sourced from
well-managed and credibly certified forests. Our paper procurement policy can
be found on www.randomhouse.co.uk

**Mixed Sources**
Product group from well-managed
forests and other controlled sources
www.fsc.org  Cert no. TT-COC-2139
© 1996 Forest Stewardship Council

Printed and bound in Great Britain by Mackays

ISBN: 9780091921514

To buy books by your favourite authors and register for offers visit www.rbooks.co.uk

# CONTENTS

'The strain of men's bred out
Into baboon and monkey.'
– Apemantus, Act I Scene 1,
*Timon of Athens*, William Shakespeare

# INTRODUCTION

I like to think that the book you hold before you now, which is the companion volume to *Bears Can't Run Downhill*, follows in the great tradition of *Through the Looking-Glass*, *The Empire Strikes Back*, *Women in Love*, *The Da Vinci Code* and *The Godfather Part II*. That is to say, sequels that were as thoroughly enjoyable as, or even better than, their predecessors (*Alice's Adventures in Wonderland*, *Star Wars*, *The Rainbow*, *Angels & Demons* – and I'm sure you're confident about the last one).

But I know what you're thinking. (Apart from: you shouldn't use the word 'but' to start a new paragraph.) You're thinking *Henry IV Part 2*, *The Whole Ten Yards*, *Police Academy 2: Their First Assignment*, *Tales from Watership Down* and *The Lawnmower Man 2: Beyond Cyberspace* – all generally rather disappointing, although it's perhaps just a little harsh to group Shakespeare's imperfect history play together with Steve Guttenberg's truncheon-wielding buffoonery.

So what *have* you let yourself in for here? Well, you can rest assured it's no *F/X 2: The Deadly Art of Illusion*. Instead, you have a whole new bumper collection of pub facts explained, explored and exploded, a collection that will amuse as much as it amazes. Along the way you can marvel at Jerry Springer's birthplace

(p. 77), find out whether your ears will ever stop growing (p. 37) and feel queasy at the excesses of aphids' breeding habits (p. 35). Use this information to silence the pub bore, to confront your elderly relative's tall tales – or simply to while away a lazy afternoon when you've pulled a sickie from work.

For anyone who *hasn't* read *Bears Can't Run Downhill*, which is an extremely large percentage of the population, a brief explanation as to the nature of a 'pub fact' is in order. Occupying a twilight realm somewhere between reality and urban myth, a pub fact is a claim which the man in the pub, or the woman in the pub, will assert with total confidence, despite the fact that it sounds completely unbelievable. And yet – somewhere, lurking deep down in among the confused ramblings brought about by a pint too many, lies some kernel of truth; and it's this truth which I seek out here. Very rarely does a pub fact turn out to be total out-of-the-blue fabrication, although a wasp-free Thailand certainly falls into this category (p. 48). Instead, it is usually the result of wild embellishment which mutates with each retelling, to the point where the person making the claim has no real certainty about the origins or genuine facts involved.

This book therefore takes a large selection of such dubious claims and exposes them to the harsh glare of investigation – a process which, for the pub facts in question, must be similar to when you wander out of a pub and find it's broad daylight outside, before realising you've got to go back to work for the afternoon. The claims are grouped into extremely broad subject areas, for any attempt at greater precision is destined to failure with such vague and suspect 'facts'. NATURE remains the entry-level subject for anyone wanting to impress their fellow drinkers because, let's face it, you could make up absolutely anything you like about an obscure animal and no one will be any the wiser. Popular culture, in the form of the all-surrounding concept of SHOWBIZ, is an area always guaranteed to raise a smirk, as everyone loves to ascribe the oddest of anecdotes to film stars and musicians alike. Experimenting with the world of SCIENCE allows anyone with a few beers inside them to confidently predict what would happen when you stick a planet into a bathtub (p. 92), while a mastery of THE LAW is essential for dispensing ill-judged advice at the bar to anyone prepared to listen. It's only proper that a crash-course in HISTORY should focus purely on the most essential developments that have shaped world events: not the decisions taken by occupants of the White House, for example, but that building's colour scheme (p. 159). Likewise, in SPORTS no one is interested in records set or feats of physical excellence: we just want to know what's inside golf balls (p. 195). Finally, as in *Bears Can't Run Downhill*, I have chosen GEOGRAPHY as the place to lump together everything else, on the basis that Geography is in itself the world's vaguest subject area, somehow encompassing everything from plate tectonics to migration patterns.

While my investigations have been extremely thorough and assisted by many (see Acknowledgements, p. 247), please remember that what you are holding is not a legal textbook or a scientific bible, so don't go making any life-changing decisions based on its contents. It's simply a very entertaining and informative read, so grab a drink (or better still, get someone else to grab one for you), sit back and enjoy.

*Robert Anwood*
*May 2007*

# NATURE

## Koala bears' fingerprints are virtually indistinguishable from humans'

WHENEVER ANYONE MENTIONS KOALA BEARS in the pub, you need to make sure you're the first person to jump in with the observation that they're not really bears. They are actually marsupials, and specifically members of the suborder Vombatiformes (no, really – that's the word scientists came up with to describe koalas and their closest relatives, wombats). Having done that, hijack the conversation completely by wheeling out the above claim about koalas' fingerprints, thereby preventing the original speaker from reaching his or her original destination – which was probably the fact that koalas can only eat one kind of eucalyptus leaf (which isn't true anyway, as they eat many different varieties).

While it might be expected that chimpanzees, gorillas and other primates have fingerprints, as they're so closely related to humans, it may not be obvious that koalas even have fingers. In fact, they do have five digits on each paw, with arguably two 'opposable thumbs' and three 'fingers' on each of their front paws (plus, of course, some rather sharp claws).

Rather more surprising than the existence of koalas' fingers is the fact that it wasn't until as recently as 1996 that someone – Maciej Henneberg, a scientist at the University of Adelaide – actually bothered to look at a koala's paws (using both ink and an electron microscope) and noticed the presence of prints. While humans have markings on their fingers and all over their palms, koalas' prints, indistinguishable from humans' to the naked eye, are not so extensive, something that makes them a less profitable target for unscrupulous fortune tellers.

The presence of fingerprints in koalas, so similar to those in humans, represents an example of convergent evolution. In other words, the two organisms have independently adapted to similar conditions, although koalas are not known to have yet developed the concept of gloves – so fingerprints found at the scene of a crime could well belong to a koala.

## VERDICT: TRUE

Koalas spend over half the day asleep, so they probably wouldn't make for very efficient criminal accessories.

## Elephants hate going uphill

MANY OF US HATE GOING UPHILL, unless it is in a form of motorised transport, or unless there's a pub at the top. In the case of elephants, they are unlucky enough to have invented neither pubs nor motorised transport, and if there's one thing they absolutely hate, it's an uphill walk.

Research published in July 2006 in the journal *Current Biology*

confirmed with hard data the truth about elephants' hatred of going uphill. (Having said that, anyone publishing anything in a journal called *Current Biology* is asking for trouble, since readers can sneer at any back-issue for no longer being 'current'.) Jake Wall, Iain Douglas-Hamilton and Fritz Vollrath, whose various affiliations include Save the Elephants in Nairobi, Kenya, and the Department of Zoology at Oxford University, studied the movement patterns of a group of 54 African savannah elephants (*Loxodonta africana*) trundling around an area in northern Kenya covering 237 square kilometres (around 92 square miles). Tracking the elephants using GPS 'sat-nav' technology, the scientists found that the massive herbivores were studiously avoiding a large, isolated hill – even though it was home to substantial amounts of vegetation (in other words, covered in food).

The scientists looked into what they referred to as 'elephant avoidance', which is striking compared to the behaviour of smaller animals, and concluded that the causes were related to energy consumption, rather than other possibilities such as the risk of overheating or not being able to find water. They (the scientists, not the elephants) calculated that by climbing 100 metres (328 feet) an elephant would burn around 10,000 kJ of energy, which would require either an extra half-hour's foraging or loss of body reserves. When you bear in mind that during a normal day's ambling around the flat savannah an elephant already spends 16–18 hours foraging, you begin to see why a strenuous activity such as climbing is not favoured: like the rest of us, elephants want a sensible work–life balance.

According to research, then, elephants really do hate going

uphill. Either that or their sat-nav was broken, and it kept telling them to turn left at the next mountain.

## VERDICT: TRUE

According to Joanna Kavenna in her 2005 travelogue *The Ice Museum: In search of the lost land of Thule*, 'Hitler hated to walk uphill'.

## Dalmatians are born without spots

ACCORDING TO DOG BREEDERS, a Dalmatian doesn't count as a Dalmatian for showing in competition unless its spots are either black or liver (a dog word for 'brown'). However, 'unofficial' Dalmatians do occasionally have spots of other colours, such as lemon and orange (which, despite how fruity they sound, are basically just different shades of brown) and blue (which any normal person would describe as 'grey').

Whatever colour their spots may turn out to be, Dalmatian puppies are born with a completely white coat. After ten days or so, the spots appear and grow quickly. Even after the initial flurry of spots appearing in a Dalmatian's first few weeks, spots continue to materialise and grow throughout the dog's life, although at a much slower rate as it ages.

Now, if you're some sort of dog midwife, or were simply in the wrong place at the wrong time, you may have seen a new-born Dalmatian pup with a noticeable fur colouring. If you thought this was a spot, then you're completely, utterly wrong: it was actually a *patch*. You idiot! Apparently there's a massive difference between patches (which disqualify a Dalmatian from competition) and spots; and apparently dog breeders have way too much time on their hands. Furthermore, if you can't tell the difference between a patch and a spot, don't even bother trying to figure out what ticking, flecking and speckling are.

Incidentally, historical understanding of the exact origin of the Dalmatian breed is fairly patchy (or perhaps that should be 'fairly spotty'). You might think that they come from Dalmatia, in modern-day Croatia, and that's certainly one theory – but others have claimed origins as far afield as Egypt and India. In the US, Dalmatians came to be known as 'firehouse dogs' because they used to run in front of horse-drawn fire carriages, clearing the way and directing the horses.

## VERDICT: TRUE

There are also Dalmatian pelicans – the tasty-sounding *Pelecanus crispus*, which means 'curly pelican' – although they're not spotty at all (except when they get caught up in oil slicks).

# Flies can take off backwards

THERE'S A REASON WHY THE FLY is called the fly, and it has something to do with the way it moves around. (Early biologists clearly rejected alternative names such as the 'bzzz' and the 'annoy'.) They can be pretty haphazard in their flight, being able to very swiftly change direction – forwards, backwards or sideways – as they see fit, something they have in common with many insects.

When it comes to taking off from a stationary position on a table, kitchen surface or 'dog egg', you'd think it might be helpful to be able to see where you're going. But not if you're a house fly (*Musca domestica*). They frequently (but not consistently) take off backwards, and fly elimination experts suggest that if you see a stationary fly you should aim about 3–5 cm (1–2 inches) behind the insect to stand the best chance of swatting it, although this advice is not generally recommended for Buddhists.

Disappointingly, just as with seahorse pregnancies (see p. 25) scientists don't really seem to know why all this should be the case. Pub entomologists will cite the faintly ridiculous theory that the fly has evolved to take off in reverse 'because predators usually attack face-on'. Even more disappointingly, scientists don't really seem to know *how* flies take off backwards, either. Insect flight has been studied extensively, but a full understanding of their ingenious means of locomotion remains elusive. Many flying insects have two pairs of wings, but in the case of the Diptera order, which includes house flies, fruit flies and mosquitoes, the rear pair have evolved to become halteres – tiny drumstick-shaped filaments that function as a kind of gyroscopic guidance system, and without which the fly cannot fly. This guidance system helps them undertake the sudden mid-flight switches of direction that are known as 'saccades', and is clearly involved in the take-off, but no one is quite sure what's actually going on.

## VERDICT: TRUE

The fly also has a fascinating way of landing on ceilings: rather than rolling upside down in mid-flight first, it will instead extend its front legs out to make contact and then let its body flip under its forelegs like some kind of miniature pestilent gymnast.

## Storks have no voice

YES, BROTHER STORKS: you are disenfranchised members of animal society, denied a voice with which to rise up against your oppressors and gain the respect and rights due to you under bird-law! Well, maybe not. As a pub fact, this is meant rather more literally, suggesting that storks can't call or sing like other birds. Which is true.

Birdwatchers, or birders, often make a distinction between 'calls' and 'songs'. (It seems that many 'birders' sneer at 'bird-watchers' for being a bunch of time-wasting amateurs, while 'twitchers' are another breed altogether – specifically, birders who try to notch up sightings of as many different varieties of birds as possible – as if anyone is going to know or care whether they're lying or not.) Calls are usually regarded as short noises, while songs are taken to be more elaborate musical flourishes, although there is no clear-cut agreement on what constitutes a call or a song. Either way, the relevant part of the bird's anatomy is the syrinx, which can be regarded as the 'voice box'. While similar in concept to the human larynx, which is at the top of the human trachea (wind-pipe), the syrinx is a bone-and-membrane structure at the bottom of the avian trachea. (The larynx does exist in birds as well, but it does not house vocal cords.)

The types of sound that can be produced by the syrinx vary depending on the extent and number of the surrounding muscles, which in the case of songbirds are highly developed. In some storks, however, such as the marabou (the tongue-twistingly classified *Leptoptilos crumeniferus*), as well as vultures, no syrinx is present at all, meaning they are effectively mute. Other storks, such as the wood stork (*Mycteria americana*), like ostriches, do have a syrinx but no syringeal muscles, meaning that the only sounds they can produce are low hisses, the occasional grunt or croak, and apparently a sort of mooing sound. So the main sound-based method of communication used by storks is to rattle their bills loudly together.

**VERDICT: TRUE**

Some storks regulate their body temperature via the evaporative cooling effects of defecating on their own legs – almost certainly *not* what the Rod Stewart song 'Hot Legs' was about.

# The original name for the butterfly was the flutterby

THE ONLY REASON THIS RIDICULOUS claim persists is because there is no definitive explanation as to the *real* origin of the word 'butterfly'. However, one thing is certain: the insect wasn't originally referred to as the 'flutterby', even though some sources confidently claim that it was once misspelled in 'an early Webster's dictionary' and the new spelling caught on. Misspelled? In a dictionary? Is anyone seriously going to believe that in the middle of the chapter for words beginning with the letter 'f', there would be an entry so badly misspelled that it started with 'b' instead of 'fl', that the 'fl' was then substituted later in the same word, that no one picked it up before it got printed, and that millions of English speakers then assumed that 'butterfly' was now the correct word instead of 'flutterby'? Or was it misspelled as 'butterfly' earlier in the compilation process and a lexicographer inserted it into the 'b' chapter, and anyone looking up the supposedly correct spelling of 'flutterby' would assume it had been left out? Give us a break. Or: show us a copy of the dictionary.

The main problem that puzzles etymologists is why the word 'butter' should have become associated with these insects, particularly since there is very little evidence of such an association outside English, with the exception of some old Dutch and German word forms. (Just to avoid any confusion: etymology is the study of word origins, while entomology is the study of insects. Perhaps what we are dealing with here is entometymology.) Butterflies aren't known for their love of butter, so various theories as to the name's origin have arisen. For example, it could be that one particularly widespread species of butterfly had yellow wings (perhaps the male brimstone) and hence the insects were originally named after this similar colour. Another theory – totally untrue – is that butterflies' excrement is butter-coloured. Others say that in ye olden days 'they' used to believe that butterflies were witches in disguise, who would come and steal butter in the night. Yet another explanation is that the arrival of these insects was traditionally associated with the churning of butter, which would have happened at springtime. Ultimately, though, no one can find documentary proof of any of these possibilities.

If you want a real example of an English word changing in this way – an example of what linguists refer to as 'metathesis' – look no further than the word 'bird', which was 'brid' in Old English. Seriously.

### VERDICT: FALSE

The Butterflies Day Nursery in the North Yorkshire town of Thirsk used to be called Flutterbies Day Nursery – but had to change its name due to a dispute with another similarly named business.

## Your fingernails are made of hair

THE ONLY PERSON WHOSE HAIR bears any similarity to nails is Frank Cotton, that bloke out of *Hellraiser*. And, being metal, they're very different nails to the kind that grow out of your fingertips. Mind you, perhaps Edward Scissorhands' fingernails are made of Frank Cotton's hair… Anyway, for anyone who isn't a science-fantasy creation living in a movie, it's not immediately obvious that the hard substance that makes up your fingernails could be the same as the soft substance that, unless you're bald, grows out of your head – and, if you're Robin Williams, profusely covers every area of your body.

Toenails are, of course, made out of the same stuff, and the main constituents of hair, fingernails and toenails are proteins called keratins. Keratins are also the main ingredients of your outer skin (epidermis) and tooth enamel, as well as various bits of animals including feathers, hoofs, the outer surfaces of beaks, antlers and horns, although don't confuse any of these with tusks, which are extreme teeth. In the case of horns, scientists make a distinction between horns that have a core of bone (as in the cow, where the outer layer is keratinised) and horns that are purely keratin (a rhinoceros's entire horn is basically matted hair).

When it comes to your fingernails and hair, the general way in which they 'grow' is similar, and pretty much what you'd expect: as each new layer of cells is formed, the older cells become compacted, harden and are pushed outwards. You've probably noticed that your fingernails grow faster than your toenails, but you may not have noticed that nails grow faster in the summer than in the winter.

Saying that 'your fingernails are made of hair' is not the most scientifically robust way of putting it, given that there is a little more involved than that (hair colour, for example, is due to the presence of melanin), but it's basically true that they are made of the same substance.

## VERDICT: TRUE

Nails and hair supposedly continue to grow for several days after death – but in fact it's only the optical effect of the body's post-mortem dehydration, causing the skin to retract and thereby expose more of the hair and nails.

## A gecko's skin is so sticky that it can support its entire body weight clinging upside down to a ceiling by only one toe

IT COULD BE VERY USEFUL TO have toes as sticky as a gecko's – but if they were too sticky, it could get really annoying. Imagine if your toes kept getting stuck to things, like when you get sellotape stuck to your thumb. That problem isn't one faced by geckos, because the way their skin sticks to surfaces is not due to some gluey substance but the so-called 'setae' on their toes. Setae are little bristly bits, of which there can be millions on a single gecko's feet. So they're pretty tiny: each seta itself ends in 1,000 even more miniature 'spatulae', which are too small to be seen with the naked eye.

There used to be quite some disagreement among scientists as to the exact way in which the lizards cling upside down to walls and ceilings. In addition to chemical bonding and electrostatic attraction, one earlier theory was a suction-cup mechanism, but it turns out that a gecko's stickiness still works in a vacuum.

The world's leading authority on 'gecko adhesion' is Dr Kellar Autumn, of Lewis & Clark College in Portland, Oregon. In 2002 Dr Autumn and his colleagues reported in the *Proceedings of the National Academy of Sciences* that they had finally discovered the explanation: the use of intermolecular forces known as van der Waals forces. The ability to adhere is related more to the way the setae move together and towards the surface, than to the size or shape of the individual setae themselves – which explains why geckos are able to quickly run away or change position without

getting stuck. They can stick and unstick themselves 15 times a second when scuttling up a wall. Not only that, but the setae have an inbuilt self-cleaning mechanism.

In earlier research, Dr Autumn's team determined that the setae were even stickier than previously thought, by a factor of about ten times. A single seta can support a force of 200 micronewtons, which to all intents and purposes means it can lift 20 milligrams. Or, as Dr Autumn brilliantly put it, with the man in the pub in mind, 'the weight of an ant'. At the time the research was published, not only did he specifically confirm for the world's media that 'the gecko can support its entire body weight with only a single finger', but he also came out with the solid pub fact that 'a million setae, which could easily fit onto the area of a dime, could lift a 45-pound child'.

## VERDICT: TRUE

In 2006 Stanford University's Mark Cutkosky, who has published work with Kellar Autumn, unveiled his 'Stickybot', a robotic gecko with synthetic setae; apparently the Pentagon is very interested.

## Male seahorses get pregnant

THE SEAHORSE IS OFTEN SINGLED OUT as 'the only species in which the male gets pregnant' – although the way in which seahorses (of which there are actually over 30 species) carry their offspring is the same as other members of the Syngnathidae family: pipefish and sea dragons. Clearly there's a big difference between becoming biologically pregnant and simply carrying a baby, so in the case of seahorses, are the blokes actually doing any work, or are they effectively just swimming around with papooses?

Plenty of research into this phenomenon has been carried out, but not as much as scientists would like, because seahorses are very much under threat and relatively difficult to study in the wild. On the 'Red List' of threatened species, maintained by the IUCN (the World Conservation Union), all seahorses for which adequate data is available are rated as either 'vulnerable' (having a high risk of extinction in the wild) or 'endangered' (having a very high risk), with populations deteriorating. According to conservation group Project Seahorse, there is an estimated annual worldwide 'catch' of over 25 million seahorses, which end up as aquarium pets or as ingredients for traditional medicines in the Far East. Apparently thousands end up as dried knick-knacks: the ideal present for the person in your life who has everything?

The research to date shows that male seahorses really do become pregnant. During an elaborate, tails-intertwined mating ceremony, the female uses her tubular 'ovipositor' to insert eggs directly into the male's 'brood pouch', for fertilisation by his sperm. The embryos then become embedded in the wall of the kangaroo-style pouch and, as in a female mammal's womb, are provided with nutrients, oxygenation and osmoregulation (control of the equilibrium of the body's water content – which sounds suspiciously similar to claims about isotonic sports drinks). After a pregnancy of several weeks, the male gives birth to miniature seahorses, often several hundred 'fry' at a time, in a process involving several hours of contractions. Following birth, the male typically has nothing more to do with his kids, and within hours he can be back on the pull; however, most seahorse species are monogamous, with the same pair mating several times during the breeding season and sometimes over many breeding seasons.

Scientists don't have any concrete explanations as to *why* syngnathids reproduce in this way. Biologists like to talk about the notion of 'investment': normally females have already 'invested' relatively heavily in the creation of eggs, so it makes sense for the female to carry the embryos. However, because the male seahorse fertilises the eggs within his brood pouch, he can be absolutely certain that he's the father – potentially an evolutionary benefit and one that rules out any soap opera-style revelations – and so biologists believe the male seahorse may have adapted accordingly. At least, that's what they thought until research published in 2007 by London's Institute of Zoology revealed that the male of the yellow seahorse does release sperm into the surrounding sea water (like other fish) before fertilisation takes place. The researchers also found that there are two different kinds of sperm, one of which seems to be an obsolete hangover from a previous means of reproduction.

## VERDICT: TRUE

It is not known whether male seahorses experience sudden cravings for sea-cucumbers and sea-ice-cream.

## An apple contains enough cyanide to kill a man

'APPLE KILLS MAN', the *Evening Standard* headline would read, probably once or twice a week. The *Independent on Sunday*: 'Apple plague to wipe out all human life by 2012, experts warn'. 'CORE BLIMEY!', says the *Sun*. Except that, after the first couple of deaths, supermarket lawyers would get apples off shelves in less time than it takes to say 'Sudan I food contamination scare'. Of course an apple doesn't contain enough cyanide to kill a man – but that doesn't stop people spreading the rumour. The theory goes that the cyanide is in the pips; but because most people don't normally eat the pips, you don't realise how perilously close you are to sudden death each time you eat an apple.

Apple seeds *do* contain cyanide, sort of. The word 'cyanide' is loosely used to refer to a number of compounds, some of which are effectively non-toxic to humans while others are extremely dangerous, including sodium cyanide and potassium cyanide (both solids) as well as hydrogen cyanide (which can appear in liquid or gas form). Hydrogen cyanide gas is particularly toxic, effectively preventing the body's cells from using oxygen: if inhaled in sufficient concentrations it can cause death within minutes, which is why it was used to administer capital punishment in various American states, until California's use of lethal gas was ruled to be 'unconstitutionally cruel and unusual' in the 1990s. Having said that, the American legal system seems to generate a new ruling on the death penalty every couple of weeks, so in the near future, execution by gas will probably be deemed 'most excellent', while death by lethal injection will be 'so 2007'.

What happens is that the chemicals (specifically, the cyano-genetic glycosides) inside apple seeds – which you have to chew up, rather than swallow whole, if you really want to try for a 'cyanide buzz' – lead to the release of hydrogen cyanide during metabolisation. This might sound scary, but the quantities involved are extremely small and you'd have to be chomping hundreds of pips in a short space of time to run any risk of death.

## VERDICT: FALSE
Other sources of cyanogenetic glycosides include almonds, cherries, apricots and cassava (which can produce so much cyanide that it can actually be toxic if not cooked).

## There's only one animal that can open Brazil nuts

YOU MAY NEVER HAVE STOPPED to ponder what Brazil nuts look like 'in the wild' (which is more often Bolivia than Brazil), but you've probably noticed that they're quite a tough nut to crack – especially if you want to get at the whole thing without it becoming a splintered mess of shell and nut shards. The nuts themselves are lodged like orange segments inside a woody, coconut-style capsule, which is technically the *fruit* of the tree. Rather than the shells of what we know as the Brazil nuts packed inside (the seeds of the fruit), it's actually the hard outer casing of the container, with a thickness of about 12 millimetres (half an inch), that proves so elusive for the hungry inhabitants of the South American rainforests.

Brazil nut trees – *Bertholletia excelsa* – can grow as high as 50 metres (160 feet), with the fruit capsules (of which there may be 200–400 per tree) often remaining up there for well over a year before being fully developed and finally falling to the forest floor. In fact, the fruit is so heavy, sometimes over 1 kilogram (2.2 pounds), that harvesters usually wait until most have fallen, rather than risk being crushed to death beneath a fruit-and-nut hailstorm.

However, if the harvesters wait too long, they may be beaten to it by agoutis – rodents of the *Dasyprocta* genus which look a bit like guinea-pigs and which confusingly are not the same as pacas, even though pacas are members of the *Agouti* genus and agoutis aren't. But if you hadn't heard of agoutis or pacas to start with, this terminological confusion is unlikely to trouble you.

Clearly, humans can also get into Brazil nut pods, but what

about other 'real' animals? Elephants could probably open the capsules by standing on them, but as inhabitants of Africa and Asia they are hardly likely to be foraging around the forests of the Amazon. Macaws frequently hack into the fruit with their beaks, but only in the early stages while the casing is still soft. Agoutis alone have what it takes (sharp teeth, agility and strong muscles) to gnaw into the pods; they will then crack open and eat some of the nuts before 'scatter-hoarding' the remainder by burying them at various nearby sites for later snacking. Unfortunately, while they're smart enough to get into the pod, they're too stupid to remember where they've buried half of their stash – a fact that is essential for the growth of new Brazil nut trees.

There is a rumour that capuchin monkeys smash open mature Brazil nut pods using stones – evidence of a rather impressive level of intelligence which has been scientifically observed when it comes to palm nuts, but which remains anecdotal in the case of Brazil nuts – and anyway, 'using tools' is cheating.

**VERDICT: TRUE**
Brazil nuts are radioactive.

## Alligators can climb trees

ALLIGATORS ARE GREAT PUB ANIMALS, because most people don't encounter them on a day-to-day basis, meaning that you can make up anything you like about them (e.g. their eyes glow red in the dark) and people will be none the wiser, and indeed very much the stupider. That is, of course, unless you live somewhere like

Florida, where they breed huge quantities of them for use in Bond movies; in fact, alligators are so common in Florida that the locals probably compensate by inventing pub facts about hedgehogs.

Apart from the lower Yangtze River, where the critically endangered Chinese alligator lives, America is the only country where you can find alligators in the wild, and then mostly in states that, like Florida, have coastlines bordering the Gulf of Mexico. Incidentally, if you're seeking a tie-break question for a pub quiz, you could do worse than ask for the correct spelling of the American alligator's scientific name: *Alligator mississippiensis*.

Enough about spelling – what about climbing? Except when agitated, the alligator seems to be a very 'flat' creature: coasting along horizontally, snout out of the water, and occasionally scurrying along a bit of mud before taking the rest of the afternoon off to bask in the sun. But they do climb fences, using their sharp claws and strong tails: the US Department of Agriculture's National Wildlife Research Center recommends that if you want to keep alligators out (or in), you should rely on at least 1.5 metres (5 feet) of sturdy fence to be on the safe side, and walls next to waterways should extend at least 1 metre (3 feet) above the high-water mark. Although they're not often spotted shinning up trees, alligators (especially younger ones) can sometimes be seen lazing around on tree branches overhanging the water, perhaps because they're scared of falling out.

### VERDICT: TRUE

In 1987 the alligator became the official reptile of Florida, although it is currently illegal to feed (or 'entice with feed') wild alligators in that state.

## Toadstools are mushrooms

HOLD ON A SECOND: two different words, so surely two different things? Or is it simply the case that toadstools are a particular kind of mushroom?

Well, despite having two words, there is no biological difference between a mushroom and a toadstool. That's right, we might as well get rid of the word 'mushroom' and just keep the funnier-sounding 'toadstool', which conjures up a cosy image of a slipper-wearing toad sitting down to read the newspaper – even though *no one except for a fast-food restaurant would ever make a stool with only one leg*. In fact, the only reason they haven't abolished the word 'mushroom' is to maintain backwards-compatibility for lame jokes about having so many *funghi* on your pizza that there's not 'mushroom' left for anything else.

In everyday speech, the word 'toadstool' is often used to mean any *poisonous* variety of mushroom, but from a scientific point of view the distinction is not made, since there is so much historical confusion between 'toadstools' that turn out to be safe to eat and 'mushrooms' that turn out to be deadly. So people who need to avoid being sued tend to use the words 'edible' and 'inedible' before any usage of the word 'mushroom'.

While we're at it, is there any difference between toads and frogs? Again, the everyday distinction between 'frogs' (slimy water-lovers) and 'toads' (warty land-lubbers) isn't biologically sustained and technically any toad is actually a type of frog – so you could probably get away with calling a mushroom a 'frogchair'. However, if you're a real pedant, you could also go round boring people about 'true toads', the Bufonidae family, of which the *Bufo* genus is the most common.

**VERDICT: TRUE**
Fungi are more closely related to humans than to plants.

## Aphids only have female babies

THERE ARE SEVERAL THOUSAND SPECIES of aphid, whose behaviours of course vary, but generally when it comes to reproduction, they are extremely weird creatures.

At different times in the year, females can be viviparous, where they give birth to live babies, and oviparous, where they give birth to eggs from which babies hatch. The females can, and mainly do, reproduce via parthenogenesis. This might sound like a Phil Collins prog-rock tribute band, but it basically means that the females reproduce asexually, without the need for fertilisation from male aphids. They can reproduce in this way at an incredible rate. René de Réaumur (the wasp paper guy – see p. 50) is said to have established that if all the descendants of a single aphid were to survive and were arranged into a four-abreast formation (perhaps to create some kind of massive insect army), they would stretch into a line longer than the equator.

To be fair, Réaumur's calculation may be apocryphal, but he clearly had time on his hands, and seemed to spend much of it just counting insects. In 1740, for example, he recorded a swarm of 43,008 bees, although on this occasion he doesn't seem to have speculated on how far they would stretch if moving in military formation. Still, Réaumur must have gone right somewhere along the way, as he ended up having a Parisian street – and then a Metro station – named after him. (Technically, half a Metro station, since it shares its name with the Boulevard de Sébastopol; but half a Metro station is still a better shot at immortality than the rest of us are likely to get.)

One of the reasons for aphids' astonishing rate of reproduction is the equally astonishing phenomenon known as 'telescoping generations': in the aphid's parthenogenesis, the daughter, developing inside the mother, is *already pregnant* when she is born. In other words, an aphid will actually carry inside her a daughter and a granddaughter, a bit like a Russian doll.

So for most of the time, female aphids can reproduce extremely efficiently on their own and males simply aren't needed. However, as autumn approaches, aphids seem to adopt an 'overwintering' strategy of sexual reproduction and at this time, male aphids are born. The males will then mate with females, resulting in fertilised eggs, which the females lay somewhere convenient, for example on the leaf of a perennial plant that will survive a cold winter. The eggs hatch in the spring, giving rise to thousands more parthenogenetically reproducing females and by that point the male – and the need for sexual reproduction – is a distant memory. Scientists have also found that in warmer climates, this sexual strategy may not be exhibited at all (as there is no cold winter to get through), with the result that the females just go on reproducing without males pretty much endlessly.

So while the vast majority of aphids are female, it's not true to say that they *never* give birth to males. A further bizarre aspect of their reproductive strategy is that aphids also seem to be able to choose whether to grow wings: for most of the year, the parthenogenetic females are wingless, but they start developing wings when it may be time to move to a new host plant, due to deteriorating conditions or overcrowding – an inevitable consequence of their incessant reproduction.

## VERDICT: FALSE – BUT THEY'RE STILL PRETTY ODD

In August 2001 the roof of Toronto's SkyDome had to be closed during a baseball game between the Blue Jays and the Baltimore Orioles, due to a massive swarm of aphids.

## Your ears never stop growing

SEEMS OBVIOUS, DOESN'T IT? We've all noticed old men with seemingly massive ears, which leads us to the conclusion that the ear – specifically, the outer, visible part of the ear, known as the pinna or auricle – grows steadily throughout our adult lives. But there could be alternative explanations. Could it be that when we get older our heads get smaller, while our ears stay the same size? As it tends to be old men rather than old women that people remember as having big ears, could it simply be an optical illusion caused by the lack of surrounding hair resulting from baldness? You'll be amazed at how complicated the answers are.

It's pleasing to learn that quite a lot of research has been carried out in this area, although it's also rather disconcerting to find that some of the earliest detailed research was carried out in 1935 by Thordar Quelprud of Berlin's Kaiser Wilhelm Institute of Anthropology, Human Heredity and Eugenics, an organisation

that strongly promoted Nazi theories of 'racial purity'. Prior to this, according to an article from the 1902 European Edition of the *New York Herald*, 'the systematic examination of over 40,000 pairs of ears in England and France' proved that ears never stop growing – but the story was very thin on details.

More recently, writing in the *British Medical Journal* in 1995, general practitioner James Heathcote reported on a study carried out in south-east England in which the average annual increase in ear length was found to be 0.22 mm. This study investigated the relationship between ear size and age of 206 subjects – but it did not track the ear size of individual subjects over time. Nor did a Japanese study reported in 1996 (also in the *British Medical Journal*) or a Korean study reported in 2003 (in the *International Journal of Industrial Ergonomics*), both of which backed up Heathcote's overall conclusion. In other words, while all these studies demonstrated that the older people they examined had bigger ears than the younger people, this did not in itself mean that those same older people had previously had smaller ears: they could have had bigger ears all along. Perhaps people with small ears tend to die younger?

It certainly couldn't be a case of evolution in progress: natural selection doesn't move that fast, but it could be the result of environmental factors such as pollution or diet – but the 1902 study (assuming it was not a humorous journalistic invention) indicates that over the intervening century the situation has remained broadly the same. In addition, the geographical and cultural range of research carried out (including studies of Czechs and Italians in addition to those already mentioned) means that scientists are in agreement that ears do grow in adulthood. A 1999 study by researchers at the University of Milan, published in the *Journal of Craniofacial Genetics and Developmental Biology* (you won't find that in WHSmith) supported the idea that men's ears grow at different rates to women's – although they concluded that men's ears start off growing more quickly, but then women's catch up. So we could be back to the baldness-illusion theory again.

In terms of average growth rates, a 2007 study published in the *Journal of Forensic Sciences* by Lynn Meijerman and George J.R. Maat of Leiden University and Cor van der Lugt of the Police

Academy of the Netherlands (insert Steve Guttenberg joke here) found the need to revise Heathcote's 0.22 mm figure downwards, with annual average growth rates of 0.18 mm for males and 0.16 mm for females.

To confuse matters still further, Jos Verhulst of the Louis Bolk Institute in the Netherlands and Patrick Onghena of the Katholieke Universiteit Leuven in Belgium re-analysed Heathcote's raw data and declared in the *British Medical Journal* in 1996 that the figures demonstrated 'circaseptennial rhythm': in other words, a peak in ear growth seemed to happen every seven years. However, this was challenged by M.J. Campbell of Southampton General Hospital, who contended that their apparent evidence for the circaseptennial rhythm was actually the artificial result of the way they analysed the data, and that they had fallen foul of the Slutsky Effect – but this accusation was quickly refuted by the original authors via the use of a Monte Carlo test. Who said the study of statistics was boring?

Overall, then, while scientists have not been able to agree conclusively on how much bigger ears get during particular periods of an adult's life, or indeed why (varying elasticity of ear cartilage and sagginess of earlobes are two genuine theories proposed to date), the overall finding is that yes, your ears never stop growing. Until you die, obviously.

## VERDICT: HEAR, HEAR

In 1997 the performance artist Stelarc (whose catchphrase is 'the body is obsolete') started planning how to grow a permanent 'extra ear' on the side of his head, in front of his existing right ear; having strangely failed to secure medical support for his plan, he started exhibiting quarter-scale replicas of his ear which he had grown in laboratory conditions, before persuading surgeons to attach one to his arm in 2006.

## The biggest living thing on earth is a mushroom

EVERYONE'S HEARD OF THE BLUE WHALE, which is unquestionably the biggest animal on earth, by mass or volume. The largest blue whales have been known to grow up to 33 metres (108 feet) in length and weigh as much as 190 tons, making the African elephant, which can exceed 6 tons at a push, look like a lightweight.

When it comes to the biggest organism, however, the blue whale starts to look rather small when it comes to length and area, finding itself dwarfed by an American mushroom (or toadstool –

see p. 34). In 1992 a massive example of *Armillaria ostoyae*, a species of honey mushroom, was found growing across an area of 6 square kilometres (around 1,500 acres) near Mount Adams in Washington state. The fungus is sometimes known as shoestring rot because of the stringy appearance of its rhizomorphs, which spread underground over large areas and 'starve' trees by nicking their water and nutrients. The most visible signs of the fungal system – apart from the dying trees – are the occasional above-ground sections, which to the casual visitor just look like 'normal' honey mushrooms and tend to appear during the autumn.

The Washington fungus was found to be attacking the ponderosa pines in the area; and it was the death of trees in the Blue Mountains of Oregon that led to the accidental discovery of an even bigger example of *Armillaria ostoyae* in the Malheur National Forest in 2000. The area covered by the Oregon fungus is something like 8.9 square kilometres (around 2,200 acres), making it the biggest organism by area known to date – probably. That's because it is impossible to prove that every part of the fungus really is part of the same organism, although laboratory testing so far indicates that it is all one and the same. And the fungus isn't just big – it's old, too: scientists estimate that it has been growing for well over 2,000 years, and possibly four times as long as that.

The Great Barrier Reef, off the coast of Australia, covers a much bigger area – over 300,000 square kilometres (around 75 million acres) – and although overenthusiastic tour guides sometimes refer to it as 'the world's biggest organism', it's actually a series of something like 3,000 distinct reefs, each of which contains colonies of millions of individual coral polyps. Likewise, a huge expanse of *Posidonia oceanica* sea grass identified near the Mediterranean island of Ibiza in 2006 may be bigger than the Oregon fungus, but again, it's certainly not a single organism, as it's basically a big field of individual plants.

## VERDICT: I SHIITAKE YOU NOT

Not far from the Malheur National Forest, in Harney County, is an open area called Whorehouse Meadow, which used to be exactly what it sounds like; an official map issued in the 1960s changed the name to Naughty Girl Meadow, but the original name eventually got reinstated.

# Slugs have four noses

GARDENING EXPERTS AND PUB BIOLOGISTS alike are happy to tell you that slugs have four noses, and it's a claim that has entered popular culture – it even cropped up in the TV show *Veronica Mars*, probably because it featured as one of the 'Real Facts' that appear underneath Snapple lids. But it's a pretty shaky claim at best, and Snapple are better known for their expertise in the making of soft drinks than for their educational accuracy: according to a 2003 article by *Washington Post* journalist Peter Carlson, Snapple were contacted by lawyers representing an agricultural group who were angry at the claim that 'broccoli is the only vegetable that is a flower', and insisted that mention was also made of cauliflowers. Snapple duly changed the fact – although it's probably only a matter of time before a furious globe-artichoke lobby group threatens legal action.

As for the slugs' noses: if we're being really serious here, which we're not, then technically only vertebrates have noses. Worms, for example, can smell, but you wouldn't say they have noses. In the case of slugs, they do have noticeable protuberances poking out of their heads, and it's these that are being called 'noses' for the purposes of this claim. If you haven't looked at a slug recently, which is quite likely, you might think of them as having two tentacles sticking out at the front, but most slugs actually have two pairs of retractable tentacles. The upper pair are usually known as the optical tentacles, as they are sensitive to light and dark – or to the man in the pub, the upper tentacles are the slug's 'eyes'. The lower pair are referred to as the sensory tentacles and are primarily used for smelling. The 'four noses' claim, however, relates to the fact that the optical tentacles do also have olfactory nerves, used for smelling. So strictly speaking, most slugs don't 'have four noses' but 'are able to smell using four separate parts of their body'.

## VERDICT: OH, GO ON, THEN

Some other weird and wonderful slug facts: they breathe through a single hole called a pneumostome, which is almost always on the right-hand side of the slug's body; and the radula, the part of the slug's mouth used to macerate food, can be lined with tens of thousands of teeth.

# The animals on the Australian coat of arms can't walk backwards

YOU DON'T SEE MANY animals actively walking backwards, but is it significant that those on the Australian coat of arms – an emu and a red kangaroo – should be directionally challenged? Possibly. Rumour has it that the two animals were chosen to represent Australia for exactly this reason: on the scroll beneath the first coat of arms (granted in 1908) was the motto 'ADVANCE AUSTRALIA', and pub historians believe that the emu and the kangaroo, at that time depicted with the shield on a grassy knoll, perfectly epitomised the spirit of a country that would move ever forward. (The current version of the coat of arms, adopted in 1912, has dropped the word 'ADVANCE', keeping just the country name – although the notion of progress is maintained in today's national anthem, 'Advance Australia Fair'.)

There's no real evidence to suggest that this is why the emu and kangaroo were selected; it's clear that two recognisable, uniquely Australian animals were chosen to represent the country, and they needed to be vaguely in proportion. The sense of scale was particularly important for the 1908 coat of arms, since both animals were helping to keep the shield upright: the kangaroo was in the same 'I'm holding one end of a large charity cheque' pose that it is in today's version, while the emu (nowadays standing soberly) was propping up the shield with one leg, in an awkward kick that could be described as part can-can, part karate. What was the alternative – a koala on one side and a stack of ten duck-billed platypuses on the other?

The inclusion of the emu and kangaroo was clearly inspired by the so-called Bowman Flag, created in Richmond, New South Wales, in the early 1800s. Recognised today as the first coat of arms created by the new colonists, the Bowman Flag shows a shield flanked by an emu and a kangaroo – although both are sitting on the grass looking sideways, as if disturbed in the middle of a quiet picnic.

Back to the point, though: are emus and kangaroos incapable of walking backwards? It's said that kangaroos' L-shaped legs are unwieldy and their large tails get in the way, while emus fall over 'because they only have three toes'. Unfortunately for heraldic

conspiracy theorists, it's not entirely true. With three forward-facing toes on each foot, emus are certainly less agile on their feet – and much less adept at reversing – than parrots and woodpeckers, which have two toes facing forward and two facing back on each foot, or eagles, which have three toes facing forward and one facing back. But if emus really need to back out of a tight spot they can (just like their distant relatives, ostriches, which only have two toes on each foot). In a piece of original research carried out for this book, Tim Nielsen, Assistant Curator of Birds at Adelaide Zoo, tried to get some emus to walk in reverse and found that by pushing them (gently, of course) they 'stumbled' backwards – but it's not as if they tipped over and fell flat on the ground.

The emus' dislike of walking backwards is something they have in common with most birds, and is believed to be a behavioural trait rather than necessarily a physiological limitation – it is clearly faster to move forwards than backwards and therefore, unless there is a compelling reason to do so, why walk backwards?

In the case of kangaroos, however, the physical make-up of their hind legs, with their spring-like muscles and their inability to move independently of each other, is a bigger obstacle. As a result, kangaroos are normally associated with hopping, using their tails for counter-balance. When it comes to walking or stepping rather than hopping, kangaroos can barely even go forwards, although when they need to, they balance on their front feet while bringing their two back feet forwards together. However, they are surprisingly light-footed when boxing, and the threat of a bigger competitor bearing down on them with flailing fists is certainly enough incentive for them to tiptoe or skip backwards. So if a kangaroo is pushing off from its tiptoes, it can 'walk' backwards, although just as with emus, it is a thoroughly ungainly exercise. If a kangaroo is faced with a threat, it will prefer to jump over it or to one side to escape, rather than attempt any kind of reversing operation. (There is one specific exception to the kangaroos' 'two back legs together' rule: tree kangaroos have fully adapted for above-ground life and can move their legs independently, which means they are very agile in travelling around the forest canopies of northern Queensland and New Guinea. To compensate, though, they're useless at moving about on the ground.)

So emus and kangaroos don't like walking backwards and do it very rarely – but how often do *any* animals choose to walk backwards? Well, aside from moonwalking competitions, not often; although some birds, such as New Zealand's kakapo – the only parrots that can't fly – do walk backwards as part of their mating rituals. But for the most part, just like humans, animals won't walk backwards unless they absolutely have to.

## VERDICT: FALSE (BUT ONLY JUST!)

A more obvious fact about the two animals on the Australian coat of arms is that they can't fly – although tourism chiefs may not find the symbolism of this limitation to be quite so positive.

## There are no wasps in Thailand

THIS IS A RIDICULOUS CLAIM – especially when printed on a Thai restaurant's delivery menu as a reason why the country is 'ideal for picnics' – and is so totally untrue that anyone trying to palm this off as a 'fact' should immediately be struck off your mental list of potential pub quiz team members.

Not only do wasps make regular appearances in Thailand, probably at picnics and beer gardens just as much as anywhere else, there is even a creature referred to locally as the Thai wasp, although it is more commonly known as the greater banded hornet. Scientifically speaking, the greater banded hornet is *Vespa tropica*, which you might think is the Latin term for a rickshaw.

### VERDICT: BUZZ OFF

For a real wasp-related fact that might help you in your next pub quiz, try this: the world's smallest wasps, so-called fairyflies (parasites of the Mymaridae family), are so tiny that they can fly through the eye of a needle. This probably makes it easier for them to get into the kingdom of God.

## Wasps' nests are made of paper

BEES, AS YOU PROBABLY KNOW, will make a honeycomb out of wax (as well as the brood comb, which is the area where the queen bee lays her eggs). Wasps, on the other hand, aren't able to produce wax, so when it comes to building a nest, or vespiary, they have to use alternative means. Contrary to what you might be hoping, this doesn't involve teams of wasps descending on street corners and making off with discarded tabloids, or swarming into bookshops and ripping the stock apart. Instead, they create the raw materials themselves by gnawing on trees, dried plant stems and weathered wood such as fallen logs or fence-posts, and then they chew up the wood fibres with saliva to create a wood pulp. They spit out the pulp to make their combs, and the substance dries into a paper structure.

There is in fact a subfamily of wasps – the Polistinae – known as 'paper wasps' because of their prominent nests, which usually consist of an open hexagonally celled paper comb, whereas other social wasps (such as yellow jackets) tend to enclose multiple combs in a large protective envelope. Of course, biologists never seem to be able to classify anything consistently, so there are always exceptions: *Polybia emaciata* is a polistine wasp that primarily uses mud to build its nest, and scientists believe this may be an evolutionary adaptation for a less predator-prone environment.

There are also plenty of solitary wasps, like mud daubers and potter wasps (sometimes called Australian hornets), which use mud or clay for their nests, and then there are the digger wasps, which use underground burrows; but if someone blurts out 'wasps' nests are made of paper' next time you're down the pub, they're not wrong unless they say '*all* wasps' nests are made of paper'. So listen very carefully before deciding whether it's time to mount your high horse.

## VERDICT: TRUE

Just in case you thought that wasps might have nicked humans' whole paper-making idea, it was actually the observation of wasps by French scientist René de Réaumur in the 1700s that inspired, eventually, the use of wood pulp in paper-making – prior to this, paper was primarily made from linen and rags (as is still the case with banknotes: see p. 103).

# Ants never sleep

THIS CLAIM IS OFTEN PRESENTED as a direct quotation from the American writer and philosopher Ralph Waldo Emerson, although strictly speaking, when discussing the ant's relation to man in *Nature* (1836), he referred to 'all its habits, even that said to be recently observed, that it never sleeps'. The exact phrase 'ants never sleep' appears in writings about Ceylon (modern-day Sri Lanka) by James Emerson Tennent, the British politician and traveller who became Ceylon's colonial secretary in 1845. He was born simply James Emerson, and it seems a curious coincidence that two different Emersons helped to promote this claim. The fact that one of Ralph Waldo Emerson's best quotations is 'I hate quotations' simply represents the icing on the cake.

Tennent observed that ants collectively work around the clock – but that doesn't mean that individual ants never sleep. Instead, they usually take it in turns to rest for short periods of time while the other ants in the colony keep on doing important things like lifting objects twenty times their body weight. Whether ants and other insects sleep in exactly the same sense as humans and other mammals is a topic of heated scientific debate, but it's clear that ants do have down-time in which their brains and bodies slow to a state that can reasonably be described as 'sleeping'.

## VERDICT: FALSE

When they're not napping, some ants 'milk' aphids for a sugary secretion called honeydew, by rubbing the aphids with their antennae.

# SHOWBIZ

## George W. Bush's favourite book is *The Very Hungry Caterpillar*

YOU ALMOST FEEL SORRY FOR George Bush. *Almost.* He faces constant derision for being 'a bit slow', and just when people start to take him seriously, he comes out with a sentence like: 'Families is where our nation finds hope, where wings take dream.' But has he ever really claimed that Eric Carle's classic work for children is his favourite (or even 'favorite') book?

The rumour (or even 'rumor') stems from a survey conducted in 1999 by Pizza Hut, when Bush was running for president. Yes, sadly, you did read that correctly: a survey by Pizza Hut. In the spirit of (depending on your viewpoint) promoting literacy, selling pizzas, or just *wasting everyone's time*, the restaurant chain asked the governor of each US state what their favourite books had been when they were growing up. The Texan governor listed *The Very Hungry Caterpillar* along with *Sarah's Flag for Texas* (Jane Knapik and Jo Kay Wilson), *James and the Giant Peach* (Roald Dahl), *My Side of the Mountain* (Jean Craighead George), *Tuck Everlasting* (Natalie Babbitt), *The Wind in the*

Burp

*Willows* (Kenneth Grahame) and Rudyard Kipling's *Just So Stories*.

A month or so earlier, W. had been asked by a student at Royall Elementary School in Florence, South Carolina, what his favourite book had been as a child. The future president's response was: 'I can't remember any specific books.' So when Pizza Hut called, the Texan governor had the ideal opportunity to set the record straight. Except that, as was widely noted at the time, four of his selections (including *The Very Hungry Caterpillar*) were first published when he was an adult.

In addition to listing it as one of his childhood favourites, George W. Bush – whose wife Laura has a master's degree in Library Science – has read *The Very Hungry Caterpillar* to literally hundreds of classes of schoolchildren over the years (when it comes to campaigning: if it ain't broke, don't fix it). To be fair, however, he has never actually claimed that it is 'his favourite book'.

## VERDICT: FALSE

*The Very Hungry Caterpillar* has sold, on average, one copy every minute since publication.

## Kim Jong-il owns a copy of every movie to have won a 'Best Picture' Oscar

IT'S EASY TO RIDICULE North Korea and its oddball head of state, Kim Jong-il: despite being the Democratic People's Republic of Korea, the nominally socialist country's Dear Leader just happens to be the son of the previous leader, while citizens are encouraged to sing patriotic songs with preposterous titles like

'For the Motherland', 'Let Us Hold High the Red Flag' and 'We Long to See Your Broad Smile'.

At the time of writing, such a regime is barely recognisable compared to Western democratic countries like the USA (where Mr President's father also happened to be Mr President, while citizens are encouraged to sing songs like 'God Bless America', 'The Star-Spangled Banner' and 'Hail to the Chief') or the UK (where Her Majesty just happens to be the daughter of the previous head of state, while citizens – or rather, subjects – are encouraged to sing songs like 'Rule Britannia', 'Land of Hope and Glory' and 'God Save the Queen').

On a more serious note, however, while Kim Jong-il (who employs at least two surgically enhanced lookalikes) enjoys a life of decadence – buying hundreds of bottles of Hennessy cognac every year, eating lobster with silver chopsticks and enjoying regular strip-shows from his troupes of female dancers – the majority of North Korea's population are stricken by famine, while the police state enforces draconian laws and the administration constantly threatens to launch nuclear missiles at Japan, South Korea, or anyone else they decide not to like that day.

But let's get back to the levity. Hennessy and dancing girls aren't Kim Jong-il's only pastimes: when not busy watching CNN, he is absolutely obsessed with films. He has directed various propaganda movies himself, has written at least one book about the medium (*On the Art of the Cinema*, 1973), and has had actors and directors kidnapped to boost North Korea's film industry. In addition to every 'Best Picture' Oscar-winner, his personal library of over 20,000 films includes various Godzilla movies, *Friday the Thirteenth*, lots of Daffy Duck cartoons and the entire James Bond franchise. According to the late South Korean director Shin Sang-ok (kidnapped in 1978 and forced to make many films for Kim Jong-il, including the Godzilla-inspired *Pulgasari*) the Dear Leader's favourite films were the first two *Rambo* movies. Shin Sang-ok and his actress wife Choi Eun-hee escaped from North Korean officials during a trip to Vienna in 1986, so we don't know Kim Jong-il's views on *Rambo III*, but he is no doubt very excited at the prospect of seeing the fourth film in the series.

## VERDICT: TRUE

Kim Jong-il's father, Kim Il-sung, is still technically the president of North Korea, despite dying in 1994.

## The policeman out of *'Allo 'Allo!* is Borat's dad

UNTIL THE RELEASE OF THE FILM *Borat: Cultural Learnings of America for Make Benefit Glorious Nation of Kazakhstan* in 2006, the fictional TV reporter Borat was probably less well known internationally than self-proclaimed 'junglist' and blinged-up Staines resident Ali G, another of the comic creations of the British comedian Sacha Baron Cohen.

Fans and critics are split over whether the Borat character represents an ingenious vehicle for exposing and satirising prejudice, or typifies a brand of racist 'humour' so extreme it makes the late Bernard Manning look like a *Guardian*-reading liberal. A similar ambiguity surrounds David Croft and Jeremy Lloyd's 1980s sitcom *'Allo 'Allo!* – set in occupied France during the Second World War, it either grates as a dodgy farce full of appalling national stereotypes which trivialises the realities of Nazi occupation, or succeeds as a hilarious parody of the 1970s BBC TV drama *Secret Army* and similar fictional representations of the war.

*'Allo 'Allo!* is particularly remembered for the way in which it handled the various languages that would have been spoken by the French townsfolk, the British airmen, the German officers, and the Italian Captain Bertorelli. Everyone concerned spoke with 'outrageous' pantomime accents – no more so than Officer Crabtree, played by Arthur Bostrom. The long-running (and increasingly painful) joke with Crabtree, who was an English secret agent masquerading as a French gendarme, was that he spoke atrocious French; this was represented by speaking English not just with an overexaggerated French accent, but with every other vowel mispronounced to result in 'saucy' puns and 'risqué' misunderstandings. The audience would convulse with whoops of laughter every time Crabtree offered the customary greeting of 'Good moaning'.

While the Crabtree character in *'Allo 'Allo!* bears a certain physical similarity to Borat, and both actors could be described as 'lanky', in real life they look nothing alike and are in no way related – in fact, at 16 years his senior, Arthur Bostrom is only barely old enough to be Sacha Baron Cohen's dad.

## VERDICT: FALSE

For evidence of the huge and enduring international popularity of *'Allo 'Allo!* look no further than the 2006 Dutch film *Sinterklaas en het Uur van de Waarheid* (*Santa Claus and the Moment of Truth*) where Arthur Bostrom has a cameo role as Officer Crabtree's brother.

## Brian Eno wrote the start-up music for Windows 95

MICROSOFT'S WINDOWS 95 OPERATING SYSTEM seems like a distant memory now, but at the time it was Microsoft's great leap forward, replacing the clunky Windows 3.1 with a new user interface based around the all-important Start menu, which has been retained in all subsequent versions of Windows.

Windows 95 was released during an era in personal computing when the Internet was taking shape but had yet to take off (Microsoft brought out Internet Explorer 1.0 around the same time), so much of the focus was on enhanced multimedia support, especially for all those users who had the exciting new technology of a sound card in their computers. Thus the boffins at Microsoft deemed it of utmost importance to create a unique and recognisable start-up jingle that would identify their new operating system as being 'futuristic', 'optimistic', 'inspiring', 'universal' and 'emotional' – and to irritate the hell out of anyone sitting near a PC that was starting up, as the owner looked around with a smug expression that said: 'Hey, look at me, I'm starting up *Windows 95* and I've got a *sound card* – don't you think this noise makes me futuristic, optimistic, inspiring, universal and emotional?'

So, who better to turn to than Brian Eno, the former Roxy Music member, David Bowie collaborator, legendary producer and inventor of 'ambient sound'? To be fair to Eno, he or anyone else could have written anything, no matter how great, and it would still have irritated the hell out of anyone by sheer repetition. In an interview with Joel Selvin for the *San Francisco Chronicle* in 1996, during which he revealed that the adjectives above were just some of the qualities Microsoft asked him to encapsulate, Eno explained that he enjoyed having to solve such a 'specific problem' in such a short piece of music. The resulting ditty, which starts with a relatively soothing arpeggio and fades out as a single note dings above an unresolved vocal-sounding chord, later became known as simply 'The Microsoft Sound'. The financial arrangements are not known, although a complex payment system in which Eno received a royalty for every single start-up, excluding PCs not equipped with sound and re-boots due to system errors or upgrades, seems somewhat unlikely. It is also rumoured that Eno composed the tune using software on an Apple Mac, a platform he is known to favour – although presumably he would not be able to confirm this for legal reasons.

Not to be outdone, King Crimson guitarist Robert Fripp – who has collaborated with Brian Eno on numerous occasions – was responsible a decade later for the Windows Vista start-up theme, which managed to be even more grating than any previous Windows jingle, with its four-note melody supposedly reflecting the four colours of the Windows logo and the four syllables of 'Windows Vista'. Yuk.

## VERDICT: TRUE

Windows 95 also represented the first time that The Rolling Stones chose to license their music for commercial purposes, with 'Start Me Up' being used for the TV advertising campaign (although cynics may have felt that a more appropriate choice would have been The Primitives' 'Crash').

## Dan Brown writes upside down

FEW AUTHORS IN RECENT YEARS have managed to arouse such controversy as the creator of *The Da Vinci Code*. Critics disagree as to whether his style is formulaic and unimaginative or an example of fast-paced thriller action at its best; his novel gave Tom Hanks an excuse to inflict yet another film on the general

public; and Brown's blend of historical fact, existing theory and original fiction has spawned religious debates and copyright-infringement claims, as well as an industry of 'unlocking the code' explainer-books that is as large as it is tiresome. In fact, if anyone's accusing Dan Brown of ripping off other people's ideas, they should probably also turn their attention to the originality of works such as *Truth and Fiction in The Da Vinci Code* (Bart D. Ehrman), *Fact and Fiction in The Da Vinci Code* (Steven Kellmeyer) and *The Da Vinci Code: Fact or Fiction?* (Hank Hanegraaff and Paul L. Maier) and hundreds of other yawn-inducing books, articles and TV programmes.

All of this hubbub – which makes Salman Rushdie look like a mild-mannered janitor – has continued to fuel Dan Brown's royalty cheques, with over 60 million copies of the novel believed to have been sold worldwide. As a result, he has become rather wealthy, but until recently it was thought that he had managed to keep his feet on the ground.

All that changed in April 2006, when Brown gave a talk at The Music Hall in Portsmouth, New Hampshire, titled 'Dan Brown Speaks: The Book, The Movie, The Controversy'. In between plugging the release of the film version, reading an unused passage that would have appeared in Chapter 74 of *The Da Vinci Code* and participating in a question-and-answer session with New Hampshire Public Radio's Laura Knoy, he confirmed that during the writing process he frequently hangs upside down using gravity boots. This is apparently a technique he started using while writing *Angels & Demons*, the first novel to introduce the Robert Langdon character, who later appeared in *The Da Vinci Code*. In *Angels & Demons* Brown makes use of a number of 'ambigrams' – visual representations of words that can be read from different angles, most commonly when turned upside down. He also described his habit of using gravity boots on his website, where he wrote: 'Hanging upside down seems to help me solve plot challenges by shifting my entire perspective.' If his next book deals with conspiracy theories about bats, you'll know why.

## VERDICT: TRUE

Before the novel *Angels & Demons*, the former singer-songwriter Dan Brown released an album of the same name, featuring CD artwork of an ambigram created by the artist John Langdon; the same ambigram later appeared on the cover of the first edition of the novel, while the book itself contained a number of other ambigrams created by John Langdon, who also inspired the protagonist's surname.

# Zed out of *Police Academy* made a film about bestiality

FIRST OF ALL, Zed is the name of a fictional character, and to be fair to Zed, he wasn't in the first *Police Academy* film. As that was the most commercially successful and least appalling of the seven movies made (so far, but we all live in hope), perhaps Zed would have done better to appear in the first one and then duck out of the sequels – like Cadet Karen Thompson, played by Kim Cattrall, who later enjoyed rather more success in *Sex and the City*.

We first meet Zed, who has no surname, in *Police Academy 2: Their First Assignment* (tagline: 'Watch out!'), where the whineyvoiced gang leader is vaguely reminiscent of Robert Smith, the frontman of British rock group The Cure. After causing havoc on the city streets, Zed then signs up to join the force in *Police Academy 3: Back in Training* (tagline: 'Run for cover!') – with, of course, hilarious consequences. Zed had clearly had enough after *Police Academy 4: Citizens on Patrol*, making it his final appearance of the franchise, as was also the case for Steve Guttenberg's character Mahoney.

So that's who Zed is. (As if you needed telling – really!) But the actor who *played* Zed, Robert Francis 'Bobcat' Goldthwait, probably doesn't want to be remembered purely as one of 'America's funniest crimebusters'. As well as making appearances in something like 50 films and TV shows, he had a long and pretty successful career as a stand-up comic, from which he officially retired in 2005. By then he was directing the TV chat-show *Jimmy Kimmel Live* and working on the new feature film he would write and direct (his first was 1992's cult classic *Shakes the Clown*, in which he also starred). The romantic comedy *Sleeping Dogs Lie*, also known as *Stay* and simply *Sleeping Dogs*, was shot on a shoestring budget over two weeks and premiered in 2006 to audiences who were bemused by the central premise: the main character, Amy (played by Melinda Page Hamilton), confesses to a one-off 'youthful indiscretion' involving a dog, and is shunned by her fiancé and her family. With hilarious consequences.

It would be a little harsh to say that the whole film is 'about' bestiality – Goldthwait might point out that it's 'about' honesty, secrecy and marriage – and it would be even harsher to accuse him of having been in four, rather than three, *Police Academy* movies, but in essence it's fair to say that Zed made a film about bestiality.

Just to lower the tone further, Bob Goldthwait's only on-screen appearance in *Sleeping Dogs Lie* was a cameo as Roy Orbison's 'bare ass'.


# Johnny Cash became addicted to painkillers after being attacked by an ostrich

The late country music legend's battles with addiction, whether to alcohol, drugs or large black overcoats, are well known to music fans, but you might not be aware of his showdown with an ostrich – or its disastrous knock-on consequences.

Cash's worst moments of drug addiction took place during the 1960s, but during the following decade he remained relatively clean. However, in 1981 he began taking painkillers again following eye surgery, before the 'ostrich incident' two years later kicked his addiction back into overdrive. In 1997's *Cash: The Autobiography*, the Man in Black provided a detailed account of the feathery face-off, which took place at the animal park he had established at his home in Hendersonville, Tennessee.

The big bird's big mistake was, quite simply, that it jumped out in front of Cash and 'hissed nastily' (the ostrich was apparently 'cranky' because his mate had recently frozen to death). Never one to play chicken, Cash wouldn't stand for this lack of respect and returned later with a six-foot-long stick, to demonstrate where the ostrich stood in the pecking order of his exotic zoo. He lashed out with the stick, but missed – whereupon the ostrich flew into a rage, ripping open Cash's chest and breaking two of his ribs, causing him to fall onto a rock, breaking three more ribs. By now the bird was distinctly in a flap, but Cash remained unruffled by the whole incident and, winging it, he managed to get a final swing at the ostrich's leg.

The painkillers prescribed in hospital resulted in a critical slide back into addiction. If that wasn't bad enough, when the painkillers upset his stomach he resorted to drinking lots of wine (he was doubtless thinking: 'painkillers then wine, feel fine'). Things went from bad to worse when Cash claimed to have been bitten by a poisonous spider in Nottingham, England, after becoming irrelevantly convinced that his hotel room featured a fold-down bed. Eventually he ended up back in hospital yet again, this time pumping himself full of Valium while the doctors kept him dosed up on morphine.

**VERDICT: TRUE**
The scientific name for the ostrich, *Struthio camelus*, means 'sparrow camel'.

## Michael Keaton's real name is Michael Douglas

INITIALLY MAKING HIS NAME – or, as it transpires, someone else's name – as a comedy actor, Michael Keaton is now best remembered for his two stints as the Caped Crusader in Tim Burton's *Batman* (1989) and *Batman Returns* (1992). The pointy-eyebrowed performer was indeed born Michael John Douglas in 1951, but is not related to the more famous actor of *Fatal Attraction* renown.

As his acting career gained momentum in the 1970s, the Batman-to-be realised he would have to change his name in order to join the Screen Actors Guild, who adopt a 'unique professional names only' rule, in common with many actors' unions. The name Michael Douglas had already been bagged by the leathery-necked star of *The Streets of San Francisco*, who later went on to win an Oscar for *Wall Street*, look up Sharon Stone's skirt in *Basic Instinct*, and marry the young-enough-to-be-his-daughter Welsh actress Catherine Zeta-Jones. Michael Douglas was (and is) *that* Michael Douglas's real name, even though his father, Kirk Douglas, was born Issur Danielovitch Demsky.

Michael '*Batman*' Douglas couldn't even safely shorten his name to Mike Douglas, because of the popularity of the long-running *Mike Douglas Show*. (Incidentally, the real name of Mike 'talk-show' Douglas was Michael Delaney Dowd, Jr.)

So why Keaton? Legend has it that in 1977 he was inspired by a newspaper article mentioning the actress Diane Keaton, probably relating to her Oscar-winning performance in Woody Allen's *Annie Hall* that year. He may not have appreciated the fact that Diane Keaton was herself born Diane Hall, later adopting her mother's maiden name when she joined the Actors' Equity Association because – you guessed it – there was already a Diane Hall (probably the Diane Hall who had a minor role in Cecil B. DeMille's *The Ten Commandments*).

## VERDICT: TRUE

Silent film legend Buster Keaton (no relation, obviously) was born Joseph Frank Keaton, Jr., although his father changed his son's middle name to the more formal Francis, before the boy was nicknamed Buster at the age of six months – possibly by Harry Houdini, who is said to have witnessed him falling down some stairs.

## *Donkey Kong* was supposed to be called *Monkey Kong*

THE NOW-CLASSIC VIDEO GAME *Donkey Kong* was created by Nintendo in 1981 as a coin-operated arcade game to replace *Radar Scope*, their failed attempt to cash in on the shoot-'em-up revolution initiated in 1978 by Taito's *Space Invaders*. Although *Radar Scope* had enjoyed some popularity in Japan, orders in the US were so low that Nintendo's American subsidiary asked their bosses in Japan to come up with a replacement game that could be loaded into the unsold *Radar Scope* arcade units, along with a new paint job.

The designer assigned to the task, Shigeru Miyamoto, decided to create a brand-new game – and with it a whole new arcade genre that came to be known as the platform game. While the gameplay revolutionised the fledgling video game industry and established Nintendo as a leading force in the interactive entertainment market, the premise for the *Donkey Kong* story was clearly not that original, being inspired by the cultural legacy of the fairy tale *The Beauty and the Beast* – especially as represented in the classic 1933 film *King Kong* and the then-recent 1976 remake. (The poster for the 1976 version, incidentally, can be glimpsed next to Jerry's window in the sitcom *Seinfeld* and features a now-uncomfortable artwork of Kong standing with one foot on top of each of the World Trade Center towers, holding an exploding jet plane in his hand.)

The huge success of a gorilla-based video game with the word 'Kong' in its title drew the attention of Universal, who sued Nintendo in 1982 on the basis that the game cashed in on *King Kong*, the rights to which Universal claimed to own. Even though Miyamoto agreed that his original intention had been to call the game *King Kong*, Nintendo managed to win the case by pointing out that in 1975 Universal had themselves sued RKO Pictures, makers of the 1933 *King Kong*, to prove that the Kong story was in the public domain (which, as it happens, enabled Paramount to proceed with their 1976 *King Kong* remake). In other words, Universal didn't actually own the rights to the Kong character or story, and in fact had previously proved as much in court. Legally speaking, the 1982 court action and Universal's unsuccessful appeals could therefore be described as *moronic*.

So the derivation of the 'Kong' part of the name is clear – but where on earth did the 'Donkey' bit come from? The ape that stands at the top of the screen chucking barrels down at a carpenter called Jumpman is visibly *not a donkey*. As the popularity of *Donkey Kong* skyrocketed, numerous theories emerged, all slightly different but all centring on the idea that the title was a mistaken rendering of *Monkey Kong*: depending whom you choose to believe, it was either mis-read as a result of an unclear telex, mis-typed by an incompetent secretary, or mis-heard down the telephone (a particularly ridiculous suggestion, since 'donkey' and 'monkey' don't even rhyme). Presumably in a tribute to this idea, British rock group A brought out an album in 1999 titled *A vs. Monkey Kong*, featuring a picture of a big ape on the cover.

When you think about it, if you've already conveyed the idea of an ape with the word 'Kong', you don't really need to add 'Monkey' to the front of it to make sure that gamers know they're dealing with a primate, especially since the character in question is a gorilla and not a monkey. In other words, *Monkey Kong* wouldn't really be any less silly a title. The reality is that Shigeru Miyamoto wanted the idea of a stubborn gorilla and deliberately chose the word 'donkey', given that animal's reputation for obstinacy.

Miyamoto went on to global superstardom (in the eyes of gaming nerds, at least), becoming a senior figure within Nintendo and creating many other successful games such as *The Legend of Zelda*, *Pikmin* and *Nintendogs*. Jumpman, the carpenter whose girlfriend had been kidnapped by the ape, didn't do too badly either – he retrained as a plumber and was renamed Mario (apparently after one of Nintendo's landlords), becoming Nintendo's mascot and the most successful video game character of all time.

## VERDICT: FALSE

Pac-Man started out life in Japan as Puck Man, but was changed for the American market because its makers feared vandals could too easily alter the 'P' to an 'F'.

# The Smurfs were originally conceived as communist propaganda

IF THERE'S ONE THING conspiracy theorists like, apart from the phrase 'grassy knoll', it's the idea that seemingly innocent books, songs, TV shows and films aimed at children actually conceal some kind of nefarious indoctrination into the off-limits world of adults. The more controversial, the better – whether it's sex (with the character names in *Captain Pugwash* supposedly being obscene puns), drugs (with Peter, Paul and Mary's song 'Puff, the Magic Dragon' supposedly about smoking cannabis) or pure evil (with the Harry Potter books supposedly inciting millions of children to worship at the altar of Satan). These examples are of course all completely bogus, but cases of children's entertainment being used to promote particular ideologies or causes – usually, ones perceived to be beneficial to their upbringing and society in general – are relatively common. The environmental message of Dr Seuss's *The Lorax* was so overt that it was banned by some schools and libraries for being 'too political'. C.S. Lewis's *The Chronicles of Narnia* novels incorporate many aspects of Christian faith into what could otherwise be read simply as fantasy books for children – although for some readers, *The Chronicles of Narnia* were not Christian enough: Philip Pullman, author of the *His Dark Materials* trilogy, described the *Narnia* series as 'a peevish blend of racist, misogynistic and reactionary prejudice' which exhibit an 'absence of Christian virtue'.

As for those famous Belgians who went around singing 'La, la, la-la-la-la' and smurfing all day long, conspiracy theorists don't seem to be able to make up their minds: depending whom you ask, the Smurfs definitely represent either a communist utopia or the USSR specifically. The typical 'arguments' run as follows.

*Papa Smurf has red clothes.* That's right: it's surely relevant that Papa Smurf, who is and will always be 542 years old, has a hat and weird trouser–shoes combo that are the traditional colour of communism, while the fact that *all the Smurfs are blue* has no bearing on their politics.

*Papa Smurf has a big beard.* Hey – who else had a big beard? No, not Charles Darwin, you idiot: Karl Marx! Papa Smurf has a beard, so he must represent Karl Marx!

*Brainy Smurf wears glasses.* How much more communist can you get? Even a child can see how much he looks like Leon Trotsky. There's no way the glasses were simply a stereotypical symbol of 'bookishness'. And that goatee! Oh, wait a minute – Brainy Smurf doesn't have a goatee… but he still looks *exactly* like Trotsky – and he frequently gets ejected from the village by Papa Smurf, i.e. exiled by Karl Marx, which is exactly what happened during the Russian Revolution. Well, okay, so Karl Marx died when Leon Trotsky was three years old, but it was Stalin or Lenin or one of that lot; basically the same thing, isn't it?

*Apart from Papa Smurf, they all have to wear standard-issue uniforms.* A bit like all those Soviet soldiers, and the communist idea of a class-free society, and nothing at all like the suppression of individuality favoured by fascism.

*The word 'Smurf' stands for 'Soviet Men Under Red Father'.* It is absolutely not a nonsense word created as the Dutch (and then the English) equivalent of the original French name for the *Schtroumpfs*.

*The Smurfs' society is a closed-market commune.* There are no individual possessions, only collective ones, and no money changes hands. Contrast this with the wheelbarrows of cash that are constantly being used to buy and sell property in *Teletubbies*.

*Gargamel is the force of capitalism.* He wants to make wage-slaves out of the Smurfs, and his accomplice, like that of most capitalists, is a cat.

*Each Smurf has a job allotted by the state.* Their jobs all benefit the community: Painter Smurf keeps everything looking good, Handy Smurf is the practical workman, and Dreamy Smurf, er, comes up with stupid ideas.

*There is no God or religion in their society.* Yes, Papa Smurf practises magic, but other than that, you can't get any more atheist.

*There was one episode of the TV series that backed up all of the above.* In *King Smurf*, Brainy becomes king while Papa Smurf is away, and his authority is challenged by a 'militia'; once Papa Smurf comes back, order is restored.

You probably don't need any more convincing. Sadly, of course, the creator of the Smurfs, Peyo (real name Pierre Culliford), had no such intentions for his characters. The blue creatures made their first appearance in 1958 as minor characters in one of Peyo's *Johan et Pirlouit* mediaeval stories (*Johan and Peewit* in English). He eventually spun them off as a separate comic and their worldwide popularity grew to encompass songs, film adaptations and plastic figurines, before the Smurfs were catapulted into superstardom by the 1980s television series created by Hanna and Barbera for NBC. (Apart from anything else, the idea that an American network would knowingly screen child-oriented communist propaganda in the 1980s, with Reagan at the time encouraging his country to regard the Soviet Union as 'the Evil Empire', is about as likely as today's TV chiefs commissioning a series called *CSI: Grantham*.)

It would be reasonable to conclude that the Smurf storylines often poke fun at the various ways in which real individuals, societies and political systems function and interact, but they were absolutely not conceived by Peyo as a model of communism. It would also be a pretty extraordinary irony, given the vast amounts of money generated by the licensing of the characters. The last comic produced while Peyo was still alive (in 1992, after the TV series had ended), consisted of a story (*Le Schtroumpf financier*) in which a Smurf, sent to the world of humans to look for medicine for Papa Smurf, introduces a monetary system based on gold coins, which leads to nothing but trouble. The conclusion is quite simply that a system that works well for humans is not necessarily good for the Smurfs – at which point, the whole 'Smurfs represent humans' idea goes out of the window.

## VERDICT: FALSE

Smurfs are 'three apples high' – a description assumed to be literal by English-speaking fans of the Smurfs, although it derives from the French phrase *haut comme trois pommes*, which is similar to the English expressions 'knee-high to a grasshopper', 'pint-sized' and 'like Tom Cruise in stature'.

## Freddy out of Rod, Jane and Freddy saved Bill Oddie from drowning

ROD, JANE AND FREDDY – 'RJF' to their hardcore devotees, who all tend to be men in their late thirties – rose to 'fame' on the British children's TV programme *Rainbow* in the 1980s. They were so successful with the kids that Rod Burton, Jane Tucker and Freddy Marks were given their own show, which ran on ITV (Thames Television as was) for seven years. *Rainbow* was an attempt to capture the 'edutainment' style of *Sesame Street* for a British audience, via a bear called Bungle, a pink hippo called George and, er, a something called Zippy.

It wasn't always RJF providing the songs on *Rainbow*, though. First there was Rod, Matt and Jane (featuring Matthew Corbett, before he took over *The Sooty Show* from his father Harry). Then, from 1977 it was Rod, Roger and Jane (featuring Roger Walker, who later went on to play Bunny in crappy BBC soap *Eldorado*). Finally, Freddy 'came on board' in 1980. At no stage, however, were Peter, Paul and Mary involved.

Bill Oddie, meanwhile, is probably no better known internationally, although in the UK he could reasonably claim to have the higher profile, having worked as a writer and performer of stage, radio and TV comedy since the 1960s, most notably as one of The Goodies. In more recent years the avid 'twitcher' has spent his time extolling the joys of staring at tits, seeking out shags and spying on nuthatches in programmes such as *Springwatch* and *Bill Oddie Goes Wild*.

The near-drowning incident – which sounds like it might have inspired 'In the Air Tonight' by Phil Collins – occurred in 1985, while Bill Oddie was on holiday in the Seychelles with his wife, Laura Beaumont. Fittingly for the fan of feathery fauna, they were staying on Bird Island, known for its Sooty Terns (as was Matthew Corbett). Also staying on the island were Jane and Freddy; Rod's whereabouts at the time are not known.

While snorkelling, Bill Oddie 'got into trouble', as newspapers like to put it when some idiot who doesn't know how to swim has to be pulled out of the water by a winch. Freddy, who apparently used to work as a life-saver before the logical next step of making music on *Rainbow*, swam out and helped him to shore. Jane probably missed the whole thing, as she was busy penning 'Superdooperbodypooperlittlebigalonianboogiewoogieplay-itagain'.

**VERDICT: TRUE**
'*Bodypooper*'? On children's TV? Eh?


# There's a street in Australia named after AC/DC

'STREET' MIGHT BE PUSHING IT a bit, but on 1 October 2004 Melbourne's Corporation Lane (a short alleyway off Flinders Lane) was indeed renamed ACDC Lane in honour of the band who recorded the video for 'It's a Long Way to the Top (If You Wanna Rock 'n' Roll)' in nearby Swanston Street in 1975.

Yes, you read that right: it's ACDC Lane, not AC/DC Lane with a slash or a thunderbolt, due to a spoilsport restriction imposed by the Registrar of Geographic Names, who advised Melbourne City

Council that street signs containing the forward slash character or similar could not be permitted, 'largely due to the automation of authority records and data systems'. With that level of sophistication in their software, it's pretty amazing that Melbourne doesn't boast thoroughfares with names like Collins_Street and St_Kilda_Road.

AC/DC themselves probably aren't too concerned by the missing slash, as a band who have recorded songs with such orthographically challenged titles as 'The Razors Edge', 'Hells Bells' and 'Given a Dog a Bone'. However, one Melbourne resident and fan, who writes a blog under the name of Knifey, took matters into his own hands shortly after the official renaming. He sawed out a massive two-section thunderbolt shape from a 'USE OTHER FOOTPATH' sign and then bolted it up against the sign for ACDC Lane, to make it truly an Alleyway to Hell.

**VERDICT: TRUE**

The Spanish authorities have no such qualms about punctuation, having allowed the creation of an AC/DC Street – Calle de AC/DC – in Leganés, Madrid, using the full AC/DC thunderbolt logo; just around the corner is Calle de Scorpions.

## Jerry Springer was born in East Finchley Underground station

THE YOUNG IDEALIST who helped out on Bobby Kennedy's 1968 presidential campaign; the Cincinnati politician who became the most popular mayor in American history in 1977; the no-holds-barred talk-show host who came to epitomise everything about US television's bare-your-soul-for-cash culture; the radio presenter with a politics show on Air America Radio; the veteran fundraiser for the Democratic Party who spends much of his time in Florida. Surely if anyone is all-American, it's Jerry Springer? His public life certainly seems a far cry from the most rubbish line on the London Underground system.

Yet on 13 February 1944 Gerald Norman Springer was indeed born in London, to Jewish parents who had been fortunate enough to escape from Nazi Germany. In Springer's 1998 book *Ringmaster!*, written by – sorry, 'with' – Laura Morton, he tells of his birth in London, but the book makes no reference to the rather odd location of a Tube station. No mention either, in the official biographies provided by his representatives at the William Morris Agency or the *Jerry Springer Show* website.

In March 2005, however, Springer told British chat-show host Michael Parkinson – whose bland style was the total opposite of Springer's excesses during the 1990s – that he was born in an air-raid shelter: 'I think it was the East Finchley station, is that it?' In case we were in any doubt (as Springer himself clearly was), in May of the following year he appeared on the game show *I've Got a Secret* in the US, confirming that he was born in East Finchley Tube station.

### VERDICT: TRUE

While many Tube stations were used as air-raid shelters during the war, it is not clear why anyone would choose East Finchley for this purpose, since it is an above-ground station; perhaps the real reason Springer was born there was because his mother found herself waiting several months for a Northern Line train to turn up.

## Random House got its name because the blokes who founded it decided to publish books randomly

WITH MANY DIFFERENT IMPRINTS, such as Bantam Dell, Doubleday, Alfred A. Knopf, Corgi, Century, Vintage and Ebury Press, and hugely successful authors, such as Danielle Steele, the gravity-defying Dan Brown (see p. 61), John Grisham and, ahem, Robert Anwood, Random House can confidently claim to be 'the world's largest English-language general trade book publisher'. But they can also claim to have a bizarre – some might say 'random' – name.

Random House was formed in 1927 by Donald Klopfer and Bennett Cerf, who had acquired The Modern Library two years earlier, and were looking to branch out. The circumstances of the new company's naming were recounted in Cerf's post-humous memoir, the suitably titled *At Random*. As he recalled it, the two of them were discussing the venture with the artist and illustrator Rockwell Kent, and they had determined to publish a few books 'on the side at random'. Apparently inspiration struck, and Cerf suggested the name Random House, which they all liked, and which certainly had a better ring to it than On The Side House. Five minutes later, Kent had sketched the company's logo.

Although Bennett Cerf will be remembered by many as the co-founder of Random House, he will no doubt be better remembered by many more as a connoisseur of atrocious puns and a regular participant on *What's My Line?*

## VERDICT: TRUE

Thirty or so years after founding Random House, Bennett Cerf bet Theodor Geisel (known to readers as Dr Seuss) 50 dollars that he couldn't write a book using 50 words – with Geisel's winning result being *Green Eggs and Ham*.

## Elmore Leonard never uses adverbs

A QUICK RECAP MAY BE IN ORDER for those of you who have spent too long in the pub and not enough time reading – although in truth, this is the sort of pub fact you might want to try out at a 'literary lunch', rather than while propping up the bar in your local. So: an adverb is a kind of word used to modify verbs, adjectives and other parts of speech (but not nouns), and will often end in '-ly', for example '*tediously* explained' or '*badly* written'. An adverb can also modify another adverb, for example '*extremely* tediously explained' or '*really* badly written'. Elmore Leonard is a writer known especially for his Westerns (such as *The Bounty Hunters* and *Hombre*) and his crime novels (such as *Swag* and *Mr. Paradise*), many of which have been made into successful films (such as *Jackie Brown* and *Get Shorty*).

Leonard (who has a surname where you'd expect a first name and vice versa, which may explain why he prefers to call himself 'Dutch') is known for his terse and fast-moving writing style, which you could describe as seriously hard-boiled, except for the fact that 'seriously' is an adverb. But a quick glance inside any of his books will reveal the occasional modified verb ('She was thinking seriously of leaving him', from *The Hot Kid*, for example).

The reason this claim has come about is because of Leonard's 'Ten Rules of Writing', which he contributed to the *New York Times'* 'Writers on Writing' series. These include some guidelines that would have Charles Dickens spinning in his grave, such as 'Don't go into great detail describing places and things', and it has to be said that Leonard isn't perfect at sticking to his own instructions – particularly the advice never to use the word 'suddenly', which he uses in many of his Westerns. Nevertheless, the ten rules, plus the final summary, 'If it sounds like writing, I rewrite it', provide an excellent insight into how Leonard achieves his gritty style.

Although he dislikes the adverb in general (to use this part of speech in 'almost any way' is 'a mortal sin', he says), Leonard's 'never use an adverb' rule applies specifically to modifying the word 'said'. Sure enough, you'll never find him writing phrases like 'he said carefully' or 'she said wistfully' – although in *Pronto* he gets dangerously close when he describes 'Harry speaking quietly'.

## VERDICT: PARTLY TRUE

Another writer who has raged against the adverb is Stephen King, who explained in *On Writing* that 'the adverb is not your friend'.

## The author of *The Tenderness of Wolves* had never been to Canada when she wrote it

IN FEBRUARY 2007 Stef Penney's first novel, *The Tenderness of Wolves*, won the UK's 2006 Costa Book of the Year award, which netted her a tidy £25,000 on top of £5,000 for winning the 2006 Costa First Novel category. The book tells the story of Scottish expatriates living in 1860s Canada who become embroiled in a murder mystery. The Costa judges said of it: '*The Tenderness of Wolves* is atmospheric, gripping and compassionate and perfectly evokes the snowy wastes of nineteenth-century Canada.' Rather more mundanely, they also said: 'We couldn't put it down.' You'd think that those judging what Costa Coffee claim to be 'the UK's most prestigious book prize' (although the Man Booker Prize committee disagree) could come up with something a little more original – but then again, you wouldn't think that the judges of 'the UK's most prestigious book prize' would include radio presenter Simon Mayo and fashion model Erin O'Connor.

The book was widely praised for its vivid evocations of the open wilderness of Canada, but Penney suffered from agoraphobia at the time of the book's writing. Although people often associate agoraphobia with the fear of open spaces, it more generally describes a pathological fear of public places or situations where the sufferer is prone to panic attacks because of a perceived inability to escape; agoraphobics therefore frequently have real difficulties travelling and waiting in queues, which means that having to go to an airport represents a double whammy. Having never travelled to Canada, Penney said she undertook most of her research for *The Tenderness of Wolves* at the British Library in London, and she also claimed it took over two years before she could get on a bus to travel to the library's site in St Pancras. If you've ever tried to use public transport in London, you might feel that a two-year wait for a bus is nothing unusual.

Despite the media interest Stef Penney's agoraphobia generated, is it really so extraordinary that a fiction author could write vividly about somewhere she's never been? Depending on your literary-theoretical standpoint, if indeed you have one, you might argue that it's the very task of a creative writer to convey imaginary events and situations in a believable manner. It's a safe bet, for example, that Penney has never been to the 1860s; likewise, H.G. Wells didn't take part in any Martian focus groups before writing *The War of the Worlds*.

In Penney's case, she said that it was 'not a coincidence' that she chose a subject to write about that would have been impossible to experience at first hand. As she put it: 'I'm fascinated by the things that scare me.'

## VERDICT: TRUE

Once the Costa awards were announced, Stef Penney said her agoraphobia was now 'cured', no doubt just in time for a mammoth book-signing tour of Canada.

# Vincent van Gogh only ever managed to sell one painting

VAN GOGH, WHOSE GRANDFATHER, uncle, stillborn brother and great-grand-uncle (if such a term exists) were all named Vincent, was only active as an artist for the last decade of his short life, between 1880 and 1890. Art had interested him from an early age, however: he had been taught drawing at school in the Netherlands and in 1869, aged just 15, he joined art dealers Goupil & Compagnie, where his uncle was a partner at the time. (The now-famous Vincent used to call the other Vincent 'Uncle Cent', which is probably what rapper 50 Cent gets called by his nephews.) He first worked for the company in The Hague, before moving to London in 1873 – where he lived in Stockwell – and then to Paris. In 1876, after becoming increasingly surly, he was fired. After a period of timewasting he studied theology and worked as a missionary, bringing the message of Christianity to the benighted people of Belgium. His brother Theo (who had the same name as his father) then persuaded him to become an artist, although much of his time seems to have been spent falling out with relatives and being accused of making various women pregnant.

Van Gogh did carry out commissions: he received money for drawings of The Hague carried out for his uncle Cornelius (also an art dealer). But when it came to the famous oil paintings, which he created for art's sake rather than on demand, they weren't exactly money-spinners, so he relied on his brother Theo to support him financially. After being inspired by the

Impressionists in Paris, Vincent van Gogh moved to Arles in 1888, where his most famous works were painted, and where he cut off part of his ear following numerous quarrels with Paul Gauguin.

In February 1890, he had his big financial success, when he learned from his brother Theo that the Belgian painter Anna Boch had purchased *The Red Vineyard* in Brussels for 400 francs. (To put this amount into context, in one of his many letters to Theo in which he asked for more money, Vincent explained how he wanted

to buy two beds for 300 francs, and that he would eventually pay Theo back by creating a set of decorations for the house which he felt would be worth 10,000 francs.) Shortly after *The Red Vineyard* was sold, he moved back north, to Auvers-sur-Oise, where he died a day and a half after shooting himself in the chest.

*The Red Vineyard* was later acquired by the Russian businessman Sergei Shchukin, whose extensive collection of Impressionist and Post-Impressionist art was appropriated by the government in 1918, and the painting is now at the Pushkin Museum of Fine Arts in Moscow. However, it was not the only painting that the artist sold, since we know that he 'paid' for medical treatment, board and lodging with paintings, and Paul Gauguin later recounted how in 1886 a penniless Vincent van Gogh took 100 sous (5 francs) for a painting of a pink crayfish, which may have been similar to (or possibly even the same painting as) what is known today as *Still Life with Mussels and Shrimps*. In *Young Vincent: The Story of Van Gogh's Years in England*, Martin Bailey describes a letter from Theo van Gogh to a London art dealer referring to the sale of a self-portrait by 'V. van Gogh'.

## VERDICT: FALSE

In case you were wondering, at the time of the sale of *The Red Vineyard* to Anna Boch, Belgian francs were equivalent to French francs, because both countries were members of the Latin Monetary Union, which, over 100 years before the euro, used defined weights of gold and silver to enable interchangeability of currency between France, Belgium, Italy, Switzerland, Greece, Bulgaria, Colombia, Spain, Peru, Serbia, Romania, Finland, Venezuela and other countries.

## Beck is the uncle of MMMBoppers Hanson

SLOW DOWN A MOMENT, who or what are we talking about here? Beck Hansen is a musician who mixes pop with elements of electronica, hip-hop and 'alternative' rock. Like Madonna and Kylie, he records and performs under his first name only. Hanson, on the other hand, were a teenage pop/rock group – and are now a grown-up pop/rock group – consisting of three brothers, Isaac, Taylor and Zac. Like Bon Jovi and Santana, they record and perform under their last name only. (Okay, so Jon Bon Jovi's real surname is Bongiovi, but it still counts.)

You may have noticed something there: the spellings Hanson and Hansen are *not the same*, because they are *not related*. Nevertheless, when Hanson made it big with 'MMMBop' in 1997, Isaac Hanson was said to look a bit like Beck; due to their ages (Isaac was 16, Beck was 26), the connection was made that they must be nephew and uncle.

Beck's own (and very real) parentage is artistically rich and goes some way to explaining his eclectic musical styles. His mother is Bibbe Hansen, who appeared in various Andy Warhol films and whose own father, Al Hansen, was a key member of the Fluxus art movement. Bibbe Hansen has been an actress, theatre director, writer, musician and, according to her website, 'documenteur' (the French equivalent of a 'mockumentary', which is probably not what she meant, although you never know: her use of the word may constitute an elaborate extension of self-referential performance art).

Beck's father is David Campbell, a Canadian musician who

played on numerous 1970s hits by Marvin Gaye, Aretha Franklin, Bob Dylan and Carole King, before moving into arranging – both for a diverse range of pop, rock, jazz and country acts and for film scores such as *Brokeback Mountain* and *Dreamgirls*. He also composed the score for the Tom Cruise, er, classic *All the Right Moves*, and shares Cruise's passion for Scientology.

Confusion between Hansen and Hanson may have been further caused by the fact that legendary producers The Dust Brothers (E.Z. Mike and King Gizmo) have worked on, to date, two albums for Beck (*Odelay* and *Guero*) as well as Hanson's *Middle of Nowhere* album (including the hit version of 'MMMBop'). They had to address their own experience of name-based confusion in 1995, when they threatened to sue British duo The Chemical Brothers (Tom Rowlands and Ed Simons), who had themselves started out as The Dust Brothers.

## VERDICT: FALSE

Other non-relations of Hanson include the Hanson Brothers, the Ramones-obsessed side project of Canadian rock group Nomeansno. Hanson did actually start out as the Hanson Brothers before shortening their name, whereas the Hanson Brothers took their name from characters in the 1977 ice-hockey film *Slap Shot* – characters who were themselves based on real-life hockey players called the Carlson Brothers… two of whom did actually play Hansons in the movie, with the third Hanson played by, er, David Hanson, because the third Carlson was unavailable. Is that enough Hanson for you?

# George Michael's real surname literally means 'son of a preacher man' in Greek

AT LEAST ONCE IN A PUB you will have found yourself so bored that you've sat around making a list of 'people who have two first names'. George Michael was probably followed on your list by Paul Simon, Henry James and Michael Douglas (real name Michael Keaton – see p. 66). If you were really bored you'll have moved on to 'people with two surnames' (Harrison Ford, Jackson Pollock, Franklin D. Roosevelt) and perhaps even 'people named after food' (Meat Loaf, Jelly Roll Morton, Fiona Apple) and 'people named after drinks' (Ice-T, Alice Beer, Johnnie Walker), before moving onto a really specialised topic such as 'animal-based musicians with only one name' (Flea, Fish, Seal).

Many such names are of course pseudonyms. You're hardly likely to be born simply Fish, are you, and no one in their right mind would call a child Alice Beer. In the case of George Michael, who was born in the UK to Greek Cypriot parents, his real name is Georgios Kyriacos Panayiotou. Sadly, this is a quite straightforward case of fabrication: Panayiotou simply does not mean 'son of a preacher man' in Greek.

The confusion may have arisen by someone mistaking his name for the common Greek surname Papadopoulos (as in the Cypriot President Tassos Papadopoulos), which does mean 'son of a preacher man', sort of: 'son of the priest' would be a more normal translation, but then Dusty Springfield never had a hit record with 'Son of the Priest'. On the other hand, his surname, which derives from the first name Panayiotis, does have an extremely tenuous pop connection: from 'pan' (παυ) and 'agios' (αγιος), you could refer to him as 'George of All Saints'. Incidentally, the defunct 1990s girl band, who reformed in 2006 after some sort of tedious feud, were themselves named after All Saints Road in West London.

## VERDICT: NONSENSE

Commenting on his ancestry, George Michael once said: 'I have never felt any connection between the Greeks and me, other than how hairy I am.'

# SCIENCE

## You can get tonsillitis even if you've had your tonsils removed

YOU DON'T HAVE TO BE Doogie Howser to figure out that something called tonsillitis is an infection of the tonsils. Indeed, you'd be rather disappointed if you had your tonsils removed due to repeated bouts of tonsillitis, only to discover that you continued to suffer from it.

There really is nothing more to it than this: no tonsils, no tonsillitis. You can't get an -*itis* of something you don't have. To get appendicitis, you need to have an appendix; to get laryngitis you need to have a larynx; to get arthritis you need to have... anyway, you get the idea. So why on earth do pub physicians claim the tonsillitis-without-tonsils phenomenon? Probably, and quite boringly, because it is possible to get symptoms very similar to tonsillitis after your tonsils have been removed – and tonsillitis itself is not really a specific condition, simply referring to the fact that tonsils have become inflamed and sore due to a bacterial or viral infection. So even though tonsillitis and inflammation of the surrounding area of the throat (after tonsils have been removed) may be caused by the same thing (such as streptococcus, or simply 'strep', which is probably a better abbreviation than 'coccus'), *you still can't 'get tonsillitis' if your tonsils have been removed*.

You might now be wondering: what do tonsils *do*, anyway? Well, they're supposed to function as part of your body's immune system – so if you get tonsillitis you could reasonably accuse your tonsils of being timewasters.

### VERDICT: FALSE

Tonsillitis or epiglottitis is believed to have killed first US president George Washington.

## If there was a bathtub big enough to hold it, Saturn would float

IS IT EVEN WORTH BOTHERING to consider what would happen *if* there was a bathtub big enough to contain the planet Saturn? It's probably about as much use as considering whether you would be justified in killing Jack the Ripper *if* you could go back in time to before he started his murder spree (and *if* you knew who he was). Still, since it's clearly one of the great scientific questions of our time, and since the UK's National Space Centre in Leicester has been bold enough to exhibit a model of Saturn floating in a bath, let's contemplate the details for a moment.

You might instinctively think of a large planet like Saturn – at something like 760 times the volume of the Earth – as being 'heavy', and therefore the idea of it floating in a big bathtub full of water seems unlikely. But weight, of course, is the result of gravity, so for any floating to be going on you'd probably want to position your enormous bathtub on an even more enormous planet, which could act as a stable surface while exerting gravitational pull on your water and your Saturn. If your planet – let's call it Balneum, the Latin word for 'bath' – wasn't more massive than Saturn then everything would just end up sticking to Saturn since it would exert the stronger gravitational attraction. Or something.

You'd also need to be careful about what sort of planet Balneum is: a planet like Saturn itself wouldn't be such a great idea, because in common with Jupiter, Neptune and Uranus, Saturn does not have a solid surface. Although Saturn has a small core of rock and ice, it is mostly made up of hydrogen, in its metallic form around the core, and then in its gaseous form for the rest, with a bit of helium and some other stuff thrown in for good measure. You

could then argue the case as to whether the bulk of what we call Saturn is actually the 'atmosphere' around the real planet itself – in which case Saturn, as a solid core, certainly wouldn't float in your bathwater.

However, if you take the 'visible' extent of Saturn – ignoring the rings for a moment – as being the planet, it is certainly the only planet in our solar system to be less dense than water, having an average density of $0.6873$ g/cm³. In this ridiculous bath-time scenario, though, Saturn still would not float, since its rock-and-ice core would be so much heavier than its gaseous outer layers, so the core would immediately sink through the hydrogen–helium gases and down through the water to the bottom of the bath, while the gaseous outer layers would settle above the surface of the water. (Or, if Balneum is a planet with an atmosphere similar to Earth's, rather than no atmosphere at all, Saturn's gases would start to drift upwards and away from the bath, since hydrogen and helium are less dense than the Earth's air.)

In other words, this nonsense about Saturn floating in the bath is based purely on the idea that its *average* density is less than that of water – but it doesn't take account of the fact that the planet is not an approximately consistent density all the way through, being part gas and part solid. While Saturn is in its current position in the solar system, the outer layers of gas are attracted by the gravitational pull of its core; but the minute you stick it in a bath on a more massive planet, the centre of gravity will be at the centre of Balneum, meaning that both the core and the outer gaseous layers are all pulled towards Balneum, at which point the difference in the relative densities and states of Saturn's core (a solid much denser than water and Saturn's outer layers) and its outer layers (gases much less dense than water) would come into effect. Do you really care, though?

**VERDICT: FALSE**
Returning finally to Saturn's rings, these would melt if your bath water was hot, since they are mostly ice particles.

## Almost all banknotes have traces of cocaine on them

LOCK UP YOUR KIDS! Cocaine use is so endemic in society that every dollar bill or twenty-euro note you touch is covered in the stuff, because the previous eight people who handled it before you were massive coke-heads who used it as snorting apparatus! Just accidentally sniffing your wallet will make you instantly addicted!

It's not as bad as all that, is it? Well, yes and no. Studies carried out in the last twenty years have shown that staggering proportions of banknotes are contaminated with traces of cocaine – all around the world. Research carried out in the mid-1990s at the Argonne National Laboratory in Illinois found that 78 per cent of one-dollar bills collected in the Chicago suburban area tested positive for cocaine. In 1999 more than 99 per cent of notes sampled in London were found to be affected. A study conducted by the Institute for Biomedical and Pharmaceutical Research in Nuremberg found that within days of the launch of the euro currency in January 2002, 3 per cent of notes were already contaminated, rising to 90 per cent after just seven months, across the whole of the eurozone. In 2006 Spanish researchers analysing ten, twenty and fifty-euro notes collected from Barcelona, Bilbao, Madrid, Valencia and Seville found the contamination rate to be 94 per cent. You might be surprised to find that top position in the drugs-on-banknotes league is the Republic of Ireland, where research from Dublin City University published in 2007 revealed that 100 per cent of the sampled euro banknotes were contaminated with cocaine.

Although they're not to be sniffed at, these scary-sounding statistics need to be treated with caution. Scientists can't check every note in circulation, so the percentages are extrapolated from sample sizes ranging from the representative (700 notes in the case of the Nuremberg research) to the scientifically dodgy (just 45 in the case of Ireland). Jonathan Bones, the PhD student who carried out the research at Dublin City University, said of the study: 'This is the largest sample of notes ever used in an experiment of this kind in Ireland.' Which is a bit like saying that *Patch Adams* is the greatest clown–doctor biopic starring Robin Williams ever filmed. Analysis methods are improving, too: in the case of Dublin in particular, the techniques employed enabled the detection of even smaller cocaine residues than previous studies. Most important, though, is the fact that the widespread contamination is not necessarily an indication that every note has at some stage been rolled up and poked into the nostril of an overpaid, under-imaginative TV producer: traces of the drug can very easily be passed from a single note to many others in wallets, cash dispensers, tills and counting machines used in banks.

Nevertheless, at the time of the Spanish research, the newspaper *El Mundo* calculated that approximately 142 million banknotes would have been directly used for snorting by Spain's cocaine users, out of around 900 million notes in circulation, excluding rarely used denominations of 100, 200 and 500 euros. In summary: wash your hands.

### VERDICT: TRUE

To clean all this cocaine off your banknotes would take the concept of money-laundering to a whole new level; however, since banknotes are made of cotton (see p. 103) it might not be as difficult as it sounds.

## You can use peanuts to make dynamite

THE FAMOUS EXPLOSIVE was patented by the Swedish scientist and industrialist Alfred Nobel in 1867, after experimenting with its key ingredient – nitroglycerine, not dry-roasted peanuts – and finding it to be too unstable for practical use. On its own, nitroglycerine is a 'contact explosive', which means physical movement can initiate an explosion. This idea is at the core of William Friedkin's 1977 film *Sorcerer* (a remake of Henri-Georges Clouzot's 1953 French production *Le Salaire de la peur*, itself based on a novel by Georges Arnaud), where Roy Scheider and some other blokes have to drive around the bumpy roads of South America carrying truckloads of nitroglycerine. Nobel's big break came when he experimented at his factory in Krümmel, near the German port of Hamburg, with ways to find a more stable solution following an explosion at the plant in 1866. After attempts with cement, charcoal, sawdust and *not* ready-salted peanuts, he tried *Kieselguhr*, the diatomaceous earth found in the

sand dunes around the factory. This light and crumbly rock proved just the substance to mix together with nitroglycerine into sticks of what he patented as 'dynamite', earning him a fortune and allowing him to provide for the creation of the Nobel Prize system in his will (in part, no doubt, out of a sense of guilt over the military applications of his explosives).

Nitroglycerine, meanwhile, was first made and studied in 1847 by the Italian chemist Ascanio Sobrero, who similarly devoted little of his time and energy to pub nibbles. He created nitroglycerine by nitrating glycerine, which in its pure chemical compound form is known by various other names such as glycerol and propane-1,2,3-triol. By the time Nobel had started industrial-scale production of nitroglycerine, glycerine was mainly obtained as a by-product of candle-making, and later as a by-product of the soap industry, and it's a common ingredient in foods (when it is labelled as E422) and personal hygiene products, as well as having many industrial applications. The first discovery of glycerine itself is usually attributed to the chemist Carl Scheele, who in 1779 heated up litharge (lead oxide) with olive oil – and now we're getting a little nearer to the whole bar-snacks idea. Glycerine, a colourless, non-toxic liquid with a sweet taste, occurs naturally in many oils and fats such as those derived from soya beans, sunflower seeds, corn, coconuts, rapeseed, lard, palm kernels and, yes, peanuts.

So while peanuts (also known as groundnuts) can be used to make dynamite – in the sense that glycerine can be extracted from peanut oil, then nitrated to form nitroglycerine, which is mixed up with diatomaceous earth and shoved into a stick with a detonating cap – they are not 'the main ingredient of dynamite', and it's pretty baffling as to why peanuts in particular (rather than lard or sunflower seeds) should have gained such prominence in the public consciousness as the 'origin of dynamite'. The only explanation is the pub status of the peanut: you rarely find yourself supping a pint then snacking on some lard, prompting you to tell your drinking companion: 'Hey, did you know dynamite is made from lard?'

### VERDICT: TRUE

Nitroglycerine is also used – rather worryingly, you might think – as a heart medication, for which purpose it is referred to as glyceryl trinitrate, GTN or 'nitro'.

# No one has ever been killed by a falling meteorite

LEST THERE BE ANY CONFUSION, a meteoroid is a small bit of cosmic debris flying around in outer space, which forms a visible meteor, or shooting star, when it enters the Earth's atmosphere, heating up as it encounters resistance from the air; if it doesn't disintegrate completely, and then falls to the Earth, it's called a meteorite. In case you're still confused, it may help to further note that 'Cosmik Debris' is a song by Frank Zappa; *Shooting Stars* was an anarchic BBC TV game show hosted by Vic Reeves and Bob Mortimer; and Meteor is a small town in Wisconsin.

Whether you're talking about a human being killed in a direct hit by a falling meteorite, or a meteorite indirectly triggering some sort of elaborate sequence of events like a life-sized game of Mousetrap, the problem is that there is no account of death by meteorite that has been substantiated beyond doubt as having definitely happened. There are plenty of anecdotal and wildly improbable stories, such as the theory that China's Yellow Emperor, regarded by many as the ultimate ancestor of the Han, was killed in the third millennium BC by a meteorite, the remains of which were found in 2002 in Shaanxi province. Unfortunately historians are still busy trying to prove whether the Yellow Emperor actually existed, let alone whether he was killed by a bit of rock falling from the sky. There have been many more recent, and seemingly far more plausible, examples, in which eye witnesses have claimed with absolute certainty to have seen meteorite deaths – but just because no one videotaped it and no scientists happened to be ambling by at the time doesn't mean they can all be discounted as fraudulent or deluded.

Scientists with too much time on their hands estimate that your annual risk of being hit (fatally or otherwise) by a meteorite is one in several billion, but with the world's population in excess of six billion, people certainly do get struck every now and then. Perhaps the best documented example of someone *nearly* being killed by a meteorite is the famous case of Ann Elizabeth Hodges, who was hit on the hip by a meteorite in the middle of a lunch-time snooze at her home in Sylacauga, Alabama, in 1954. And during a small meteorite shower in 1992 a boy was hit on the head by a fragment of falling rock in Mbale, Uganda, surviving to dine out on the experience for the rest of his life.

In the book *Rain of Iron and Ice: The Very Real Threat of Comet and Asteroid Bombardment*, a title that could not lead to accusations of its author sitting on the fence, space expert John S. Lewis concludes that the probabilities over the course of time and the many thousands of historical reports add up to the fact that it is certain that humans have been killed by meteorites, and that it is impossible to discount all historical accounts as hoaxes or mistakes. So while you won't yet be able to find footage on YouTube of a space boulder landing on a kid doing *Star Wars* impressions with a golf club, the idea that no one has ever been killed by a meteorite is officially bogus.

## VERDICT: FALSE

In 2004 a teacher at St Matthew's Roman Catholic High School in Moston, Manchester, announced at morning assembly that a meteorite would strike within days, killing everyone, and that the children should go home early to say their final farewells to their families; she then revealed to her distraught pupils that she had made up the story to illustrate the principle that you should 'seize the day'. (In her defence, she had probably just watched Robin Williams in *Dead Poets Society* and found his tear-jerking, over-saccharined performance so nauseating that she wished the world would end.)

## Your eyeballs never grow

PEOPLE MAKING THIS CLAIM MEAN that once you're born, your eyeballs don't get any bigger for the rest of your life. (Diseases and bizarre injuries involving being shot in the eye by a compressed-air pellet, like the one which kills Kananga in *Live and Let Die*, don't count.) In other words, eyeballs are – supposedly – the opposite of your ears when it comes to growing (see p. 37).

When you consider that eyesight can change over time, resulting in worsening short-sightedness (myopia) or long-sightedness (hyperopia), you might think that these conditions would be the result of changing eyeball size. In fact, you might think that scientists know what causes these conditions, but apparently it's still not entirely clear why the eyeball becomes too long or too short (the cause of common forms of myopia and hyperopia, although other structural changes are also causes). Whatever the reasons, you could still argue that the *shape* of the eye may change over time, but that it doesn't *grow* in the sense of developing into a larger eyeball. Likewise, structural changes such as lessened lens elasticity and muscle power may be the cause of other conditions such as presbyopia (which sounds like the notion of an ideal world created by Scottish protestants, but actually refers to the way the eye is less able to focus with age).

Regardless of discussions about shape and structure, a baby's eyeballs at birth do *not* remain the same size for the rest of his or her life, although they do start out disproportionately big, which is probably why this claim is so readily believed. A new-born sprog's eyeball is around 65–75 per cent of the size of an adult's eye; there is relatively rapid growth up to the age of about two, and the eyeball continues to grow during puberty, reaching a final diameter of approximately 25 millimetres (1 inch) at adulthood.

## VERDICT: FALSE

In February 2007 archaeologists working in Iran revealed that the world's oldest artificial eye, dating from the third millennium BC, had been coated with gold to give the impression that its wearer, a very tall woman with a 'striking and exotic figure', had supernatural powers.

# Banknotes are printed on cotton

IN AN AGE WHEN A SALARY can magically appear in your bank account without anything physically changing hands, when you can use a plastic card to buy a round of beers, and when vast sums are transferred as numbers on screens in exchange for predictions about the future prices of frozen concentrated orange juice and pork bellies, it feels almost quaint to consider why banknotes, or bills, originally came into being.

In ye olden days, of course, the concepts of 'money' and 'what things are worth' related to the physical quantity and value of your holdings, whether that was livestock, rice or precious metals. In other words, if you literally had a chunk of gold twice as heavy as the next guy's chunk, it was worth twice as much. Carting all that gold and silver around (and finding enough of it to mint coins) obviously became impractical – as England's King John found in 1216, to his immense cost, when his treasure was lost during an ill-advised crossing of The Wash in East Anglia. So the idea of bits of paper arose (initially in China around the late tenth century AD, and in Europe and America some 600 years later), either as receipts for physical coins or other stock held on the owner's behalf, or as promissory bills indicating that the issuer would pay up gold or some other commodity at a future date. Over the centuries, banknotes increasingly came to represent 'fiat money', in other words notional interchangeable values that are not, in reality, backed by physical amounts of precious metals, and do not reflect the actual value of the paper used to create the notes.

Indeed, when you think too hard about how the monetary system works, with people civilly accepting the idea that you can work all month in exchange for some digits appearing on an ATM screen – even though, technologically speaking, those digits could be quadrupled in value at the click of a corrupt banking official's mouse – it's a wonder that society doesn't totally break down every few years.

So, what about those who tell you that banknotes are 'printed on cotton, not paper'? The 'not paper' bit is extremely suspect: while most paper is made from wood pulp, it can also be made from any vegetable fibres, including cotton, hemp, linen and *rags*. And there you have it: in a true rags-to-riches story, Bank of England notes are made from a mixture of cotton fibres and linen rags, for reasons of durability – and the US Treasury Department's Bureau of Engraving and Printing similarly use a 25 per cent linen and 75 per cent cotton mix. Whatever type of paper countries choose, synthetic fibres, metal and other security devices are often integrated into the paper before printing. In addition, many countries, such as Australia and New Zealand, use plastic banknotes because they are even more resilient and allow transparent areas for optically variable security devices.

## VERDICT: TRUE

Technically, no banknotes are legal tender in Scotland, not even those issued by Scottish banks, because they are not legally defined as examples of payment that *must* be accepted; however, the law also states that creditors must accept payment by any reasonable means, which allows the usage of Scottish and English banknotes on the basis that they're generally pretty safe.

## The average chocolate bar contains eight insect legs

IT'S NOT CLEAR WHY the figure of eight should have
established itself as the supposed number of insect legs contained
in a typical chocolate bar, but whatever the reason, it has no more
accuracy than the claim that the average pork pie contains one
pig's testicle. However, you might still be surprised at the levels
of insect contamination in chocolate.

The 'eight legs' statistic may have its origins in the fact that
some food additives used in confectionery manufacture are derived
from insects. For example, cochineal – also known as carmine,
Natural Red 4, Crimson Lake and, in European food labelling,
E120 – is a red food colouring that is extracted by boiling, drying
and powdering cochineals (scale insects of the *Dactylopius* genus).
This iş why strict vegetarians don't drink Campari. Shellac, or
E904, sometimes used as a glaze on sweets (as well as being used
in furniture polish), tends to be avoided by vegetarians and vegans
alike, since the collection of the secretion of the lac insect typically
involves fatal 'collateral damage' to the beetles themselves.
(Shellac is also the name of the post-punk rock group formed by
Steve Albini, Bob Weston and Todd Trainer, whose music can be
enjoyed by anyone, regardless of their dietary persuasion.)

So insect-derived additives are permitted in foods – but
contamination during processing is a more common source of
insect content than the active use of additives. The US Food and
Drug Administration (FDA) publishes a list of 'food defect action
levels', which detail 'levels of natural or unavoidable defects in
foods for human use that present no health hazard'. In other

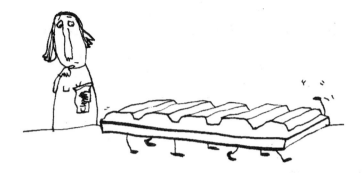

words, levels that are acceptable and deemed to be the upper limits safe for consumption. In the case of chocolate, the action level for 'insect filth' (a technical term, apparently) is an average of '60 or more insect fragments per 100 grams when 6 100-gram subsamples are examined' or where 'any 1 subsample contains 90 or more insect fragments'.

The FDA guidelines state that the action level figures refer to sample averages when testing for conformity. In other words, these are not averages actually found across the food industry, which are much lower for the foods concerned, at around roughly 10 per cent of the action levels. This would mean an average 100-gram sample might contain around six insect fragments, so a 50-gram chocolate bar might contain around three. A 2001 study of eight samples conducted by the Central Hudson Laboratory, who specialise in, among other areas, 'insect fragment and rodent hair analysis and interpretations', found an average of 14.4 insect fragments per 225-gram sample, which works out as an average of 3.2 fragments per 50 grams – consistent with the calculations based on 10 per cent of the FDA action levels. To keep a sense of perspective, however, don't forget that these fragments are simply that – fragments – and not whole insect legs. So it's not like you're eating some kind of insect can-can every time you give in to the temptation of chocolate.

**VERDICT: FALSE**
A Californian company called Hotlix (phone number 1-800-EAT-WORM) sells ant-filled chocolate wafers and chocolate-dipped worms and crickets, although none of these could reasonably be regarded as 'the average chocolate bar'.

# All sand dunes have a slope of 34°

You might think that such a specific figure of 34° would relegate this claim to a dry-as-the-desert physics textbook, rather than something worthy of astounding your fellow drinkers, but it is saved as a 'pub fact' by virtue of the word 'all': any sentence starting with the word 'all' can be used with confidence in a pub environment, because it cuts through unnecessary details and counter-examples to get right to the most generalised claim possible. In this case, do *all* sand dunes have exactly the same slope, regardless of wind conditions, location and other factors?

Actually, what is meant by 'slope' here? In order to understand this, we have to consider how sand dunes are created (not the most exciting prospect, let's be honest). Even though some of the world's oldest civilisations, such as the Egyptians and the Persians, were no strangers to dunes, it wasn't until the twentieth century that anyone could be bothered to look in detail at how they are formed. The man credited with first formulating a thorough scientific explanation was British Army officer Ralph Bagnold (whose sister Enid wrote *National Velvet*). Following his experiences in the deserts of the Middle East and North Africa between the 1920s and 1940s, including his founding of the Army's Long Range Desert Group during the Second World War, he acquired an expert understanding of desert conditions and sand movement, with his best-known work being *The Physics of Blown Sand and Desert Dunes*, published in 1941. Bagnold and the researchers who followed him established that there are three key ways in which wind causes sand to form dunes: 'suspension', in which finer grains of sand are suspended in the air and carried relatively long distances; 'saltation', in which heavier grains of sand are blown up by the wind, fall back to the ground, and then bounce up again; and 'impact creep' or 'surface creep', in which these bouncing grains hit other grains on the ground, moving them forward in turn.

As the wind piles the sand up, the grains continue to be shifted up the windward side of the dune to the top of the heap, until the back of the dune (the leeward side) becomes so steep it collapses. Therefore the leeward side is often referred to as the 'slip-face' – and the 'slope' in the context of the 34° claim is the angle of the slip-face. Although dunes keep moving in the direction of the wind, with the slip-face continually collapsing and inching along, the factor that determines the incline of the slip-face is referred to as the angle of repose – the angle at which the pile of sand can stabilise, but beyond which it will collapse again by slipping, shearing, slumping (all very different processes, in case you were wondering) or avalanching.

In the majority of sand dunes – including those on Mars – this angle really is 34°. However, in news that will disappoint any pub physicist, the angle of repose can vary slightly depending on the composition of the sand, and can sometimes be as low as 30° (although it does not seem ever to be higher than 34°). In a further blow, there are some rare dune shapes – domes – in which there is no slip-face at all.

**VERDICT: VERY NEARLY**

Some sand dunes can 'sing' noises similar to drum rolls, organs, galloping horses and jet aeroplanes, due to the combination of a coating of silicon, iron and manganese on certain grains and the synchronisation of grains resonating together when the sand avalanches down the slip-face.

# The guy who invented Celsius got the scale the wrong way round

YOU MIGHT NOT BE TOO amazed to discover that 'the guy who invented Celsius' was Anders Celsius, although the temperature scale we know today was not officially named Celsius until 1948, before which it was mostly referred to as 'degrees centigrade' or 'centesimal degrees'. Unless of course you live in the US, in which case you've probably never heard of Celsius and are now reeling from the shock that the rest of the world views the Fahrenheit system as obsolete.

Celsius spent most of his time studying astronomy, but today he is best remembered for the creation of a temperature scale divided

into 100 units between the freezing and boiling points of water. The Swede wasn't the first to invent a system for measuring temperature – but he was the first to attempt the creation of an international standard scale by carrying out rigorous scientific experiments. Specifically, his explanations and predictions of the effects of atmospheric pressure on the boiling point of water were very accurate, and when he proposed his temperature scale in 1742 he determined that 0° should be the boiling point of water at mean barometric pressure at mean sea level. The opposite end of the scale – 100° – would be the freezing point, meaning that on the original Celsius scale, the degrees rose as the temperature cooled.

The reversal of the scale after Celsius's death in 1744 wasn't the result of some bungling short-sighted professor mistakenly reading something the wrong way up, but it's not known for certain who was responsible for the deliberate switch, with various candidates including Mårten Strömer (Celsius's successor as Chair of Astronomy at Uppsala University), and the instrument maker Daniel Ekström. What is clear is that Carolus Linnaeus (better known for his work on biological classification and naming conventions) was keen to record detailed temperature measurements at the newly restored botanical gardens in Uppsala. He ordered a thermometer from Ekström that was ready in 1744, but which broke in transit, before a second one arrived in late 1745, and in December that year Linnaeus published *Hortus Upsaliensis*, which features the first-ever description of a thermometer with 0° for water's freezing point and 100° for water's boiling point.

## VERDICT: TRUE

Although the whole idea behind Celsius's scale was the use of the two fixed points represented by the temperatures at which water boils and freezes, when scientists came to rationalise Celsius with the more modern Kelvin scale they changed the reference points of Celsius to be absolute zero (zero on the Kelvin scale, or −273.15°C) and the 'triple point' of water (the point at which water can coexist as a gas, liquid and solid in thermodynamic equilibrium – very nearly, but not exactly, the traditional notion of the freezing point). The upshot is that technically speaking, the boiling point of water under one standard atmosphere of pressure is now just slightly lower than 100°C.

# There's a gene named after Sonic the Hedgehog

SEGA'S SONIC THE HEDGEHOG is one of the world's most recognisable video game characters, alongside Nintendo's Mario, Namco's Pac-Man and Eidos Interactive's Lara Croft, of the *Tomb Raider* series. Ever since his first appearance in 1991, the little blue creature has been battling Dr Eggman (also known as Dr Robotnik), in numerous games such as *Sonic the Hedgehog*, *Sonic Adventure*, *Sonic Heroes*, *Sonic Advance* and *Sonic and the Secret Rings*, as well as appearing in various related titles such as *Sonic Riders*, *Sonic Shuffle* and *Sonic Pinball Party*, and his multimedia empire encompasses comics and animated TV series. When not busy shuffling and partying, he's also apparently running around in your body, because there is a gene called Sonic Hedgehog (symbol: SHH).

The frivolous-sounding name does not mean that SHH is some obscure protein that geneticists don't really bother with; on the contrary, it has been widely studied and plays an important role in human tissue development.

Sonic Hedgehog is one of three homologues (equivalent genes in mammals) of an original Hedgehog gene that was first identified in fruit flies during the 1970s by Christiane Nüsslein-Volhard and Eric F. Wieschaus, who were later awarded the Nobel Prize in Physiology or Medicine for their work. The original protein was so named because of the fact that mutations in the gene caused some fruit fly larvae to be stubby in shape and covered in a solid patch of spiky denticles (rather than being long and thin, with regular bands of denticles).

As researchers sought equivalent genes to help explain how the human embryo develops, they first identified two homologues which they named after species of hedgehog: Desert Hedgehog (DHH) and Indian Hedgehog (IHH). When a third homologue was discovered by Cliff Tabin's team at Harvard Medical School in the 1990s, it was originally to be called the Common European Hedgehog. However, Tabin's colleague Robert Riddle, who had first cloned the gene, asked for it to be named after the video game character, apparently after seeing it in his daughter's copy of the British *Sonic the Comic* magazine. Those wacky scientists – the next thing you know, they'll be wearing Daffy Duck socks!

## VERDICT: TRUE

The video game character got his name because he can run faster than the speed of sound and because, er, he's a hedgehog (albeit one who wears gloves and doesn't look anything like a hedgehog).

# In Germany they used to predict the weather with frogs

WHO CARES WHAT THE WEATHER'S going to be like? Yes, in the longer term, future weather trends over years and decades are of interest, and some of the predictions about global warming are more than a little alarming, but when it comes to what it's going to be like later on today and tomorrow, really, who cares? It's going to rain. Well, you still have to go to work. It's going to be sunny. It doesn't change the fact that you have to drive over to Aunt Patricia's to pick up that camera she borrowed while you were away on business. Yes, the weather forecast might affect whether you take an umbrella or your sunglasses, but seriously, does that justify the five minutes of insufferable blather about occluded fronts that seems to round off every news bulletin?

Not to mention the sponsorship. Yeah, sponsor the weather, great idea. And use a slogan, any slogan, as long as it ends in the unimaginative 'whatever the weather'. 'Acme Toasters: brightening your breakfast, whatever the weather'; or 'Acme Cars: comfort and safety, whatever the weather.' We get the idea. *Think up something else, you lazy advertisers, just for once.* The sponsorship

takes up as much time – and is as irritating and useless as – the weather itself.

Admittedly, if you're a farmer, sailor or gardener or you live in a hurricane zone, you may feel rather differently. In which case, when they do finally scrap weather forecasts, you might turn to any number of animals that can predict changes in the weather, especially if you live in Florida, where hurricanes are obviously quite a concern. In 2004 scientists at the University of Florida in Gainesville noticed butterflies taking shelter several hours before Hurricane Jeanne hit the city. As Tropical Storm Gabrielle approached the Florida coastline in 2001, scientists at Mote Marine Laboratory observed that all thirteen blacktip sharks they were monitoring in Terra Ceia Bay abruptly headed out to the open waters to avoid the storm's path. When Hurricane Andrew struck a power plant in Miami-Dade County in 1992, all the crocodiles living in the plant's cooling canals survived – but biologists don't know how. Alligators, on the other hand, aren't quite so smart: after a hurricane passed over Lake Okeechobee in 2004, a large number of dead alligators were found washed up on the shore – probably because they were hiding in trees (see p. 31).

Scientists believe that some animals' apparent ability to sense imminent changes in the weather is the result of detecting variations in air pressure: a drop in pressure usually signals bad weather, so the animal takes some kind of action to keep out of trouble, whether that's fleeing, hiding or (in the case of some bird species) delaying migration to a particular area. With dolphins and other sea creatures, in addition to the knock-on effect of decreasing air pressure affecting water pressure, changes in the ocean's salt levels and disturbance caused by distant heavy rainfall may also play a role.

So what about frogs? At least two centuries after Evangelista Torricelli's 1643 invention of the mercury barometer should have made them redundant, frogs really were still being used as early-warning systems in various countries, because certain species start croaking furiously, climbing downwards or burrowing under-ground when the air pressure drops. The use of frogs was particularly widespread in Germany, where the word *Wetterfrosch* ('weather frog') emerged specifically to denote a type of barometer in which a tree-frog would climb up and down a small wooden ladder in a glass jar: the higher up the ladder the frog was, the better the weather was going to be. The word *Wetterfrosch* is used in Germany to this day as an alternative word for *Laubfrosch* (the European tree-frog), as well as an informal term for a weatherman.

## VERDICT: TRUE

At the 1851 Great Exhibition in London, the improbably named George Merryweather displayed his Tempest Prognosticator, a bizarre device in which a 'jury' of twelve leeches were placed into water-filled glass jars; when the air pressure dropped, one or more leeches would climb out of their jars, thereby knocking pieces of whalebone out of position, which in turn caused hammers to strike a bell.

# The average American male has half a pound of kidney beans in his guts when he dies

IT'S DIFFICULT TO READ THAT with a straight face, isn't it? Yet this claim is out there, circulating 'in the wild'. Anyone who reckons they can get away with this as 'definitely true, honestly I read it somewhere' is banking on the fact that you're not likely to be in a position to check every American male's post-mortem report from the last year to take an average, even if a typical post-mortem examination would result in a figure relating to the quantity of kidney beans found in the deceased's guts. Which it wouldn't.

Common sense and figures on actual bean consumption are surely all you need to discredit this ludicrous claim. Who better to turn to than the US Dry Bean Council? Made up of representatives across the bean industry, including growers, processors and canners, the organisation's goal is 'educating U.S. consumers about the benefits of beans' – an aim that is achieved via their Bean Education & Awareness Network, or B.E.A.N. for short. (Do you see what they've done there?)

According to the US Dry Bean Council, the actual consumption of beans by Americans falls well short of the levels recommended in the *Dietary Guidelines for Americans* (published every five years by the US Department of Agriculture and the US Department of Health & Human Services). The 2005 edition recommends that Americans eat three cups a week of dry beans – which could include pintos, limas, garbanzos and other bean varieties as well as kidney beans. The US Dry Bean Council say that while this would mean a consumption per person of 26 pounds (11.8 kg) per year, the latest available figures show that in reality Americans consume just 7.4 pounds (3.4 kg) of dry beans per year. That's 7.4 pounds *per year*, which on average is 0.32 ounces (a little over 9 grams) a day.

Let's assume that the contents of the average American's guts are, to put it politely, replaced each day. Let's also assume, generously, that this average American eats only kidney beans and not pintos or any other kind of dry bean. When that average American ends up on the mortuary slab, why would they on average have half a pound (8 ounces, or 227 grams) of kidney beans in their guts, compared to the average daily amount of 0.32 ounces? Even if you assume – without any evidence – that American males eat ten times as many kidney beans as American females, it still doesn't make any sense. Of course, we're talking averages here, so it's not like the average American divides up their kidney bean consumption into precisely 0.32 ounces per day – but we're averaging out the contents found in post-mortem gut examinations too, remember?

If the half-pound-of-beans-in-guts statistic were actually true, perhaps an explanation might be that eating a large amount of kidney beans is likely to kill you. In other words, the 'average' American male who ends up dying is a massive kidney bean fan, while the rest of the population tend not to die so soon. Or something like that. Even if you can make that scenario work statistically, the US Dry Bean Council aren't going to back you up.

## VERDICT: FALSE

In March 2007 drug enforcement officers in New York City smashed a Colombian drug cartel who had smuggled $24 million worth of heroin into the country inside hollowed-out kidney beans; half a pound of those and you'd definitely end up dead.

## Hot water is heavier than cold water

ISN'T THE WHOLE POINT about hot water that it rises? And doesn't it rise because it's lighter? When you heat water in a pan on the hob, the heat source beneath the pan causes the water to rise, with the cooler water then falling and itself getting heated up – that's an example of forced convection, isn't it? In other words, it's more efficient to heat from the bottom, to avoid the hot water staying at the top with the bottom of the pan staying cold. You don't *grill water*, do you? Well, true, but this pub fact basically encapsulates the everyday confusion between notions of weight, mass, density and volume, and the fact that unless you were listening very closely at school, you may not be aware of the special properties of water when it reaches 4°C (39.2°F).

Let's start clearing up the confusion by ruling out ice. We all know that ice is frozen water and that it floats – meaning it must be 'lighter' than warmer water; but for the purposes of this pub fact, it's fair to assume that the cold versus hot issue refers to water in its liquid state. Similarly, let's restrict the situation to fresh water of a typical purity; it's common for warm sea water to sink below colder water due to the effects of salinity levels.

Now for the whole density thing. Generally speaking, as water gets hotter, it becomes less dense. What that means is that the same volume of water will have a lower mass at a higher temperature. In other words, if you fill a litre bottle with water that has a

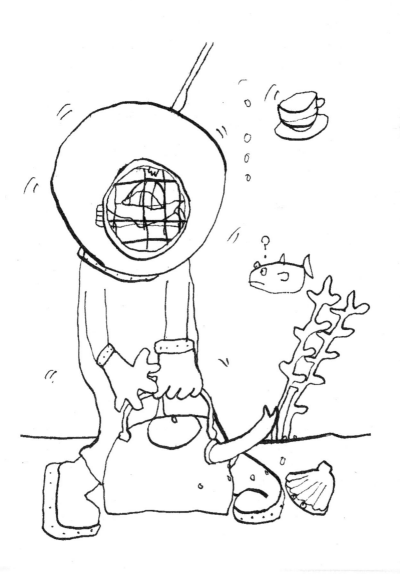

temperature of 10°C (50°F) and can be bothered to stick it on some scales, you'll find that it weighs more (by about 4 grams, or 0.14 ounces) than the same bottle filled with water that has a temperature of 30°C (86°F). Which means that in pub terms, hot water is *lighter* than cold water. Hence the whole pan-on-the-hob business.

However, for some reason (which will not be entered into here, due to limitations of boredom) water reaches its maximum density at 4°C (39.2°F). Therefore, as hot water cools down towards 4°C it gets gradually 'heavier', but as it cools further from 4°C (39.2°F) down towards 0°C (32°F) its density *decreases* again – or to put it another way, it starts getting lighter again. This means that there is a narrow range of comparative temperatures for which hotter water could be said to be 'heavier than cold water': for example, a litre of water at 6°C (42.8°F) will weigh slightly more (by about 0.04 grams, or 0.0014 ounces) than a litre of water at 1°C (33.8°F). But for any temperature higher than about 8.2°C (46.8°F) water will be 'lighter' than water of any lower temperature.

This oddity explains why in a frozen pond, fish can 'chill out' in a non-frozen bit at the bottom, because the near-freezing parts of the water actually rise above the very slightly warmer parts that end up at the bottom. Of course, if your pond is in outer space – in some sort of aquarium contained within a plastic sphere to keep some air inside for life to be sustained – then the cold and hot bits won't rise or fall at all, because although the water will vary in density according to temperature in the same way, the lack of gravitational pull would mean the water, while having mass, won't weigh anything, meaning that none of the water is 'heavier' than other parts. In fact, if you've managed to sort out the means to construct such a pond, you would probably be carrying out more interesting experiments, like seeing how much cash you can fleece out of gullible space tourists or trying to float Saturn in a bathtub (see p. 92).

## VERDICT: SOMETIMES

If you want to make ice cubes in your freezer, and you've left your party preparations to the last minute, you may find it useful to know that hot water will freeze more quickly than cold water.

# THE LAW

## It's illegal to drive in bare feet

IT DOESN'T MATTER WHAT country you go to: this claim seems to be extraordinarily widespread. Should you ever bother to challenge anyone on the matter, their 'evidence' tends to be along the lines of 'I used to go out with a driving instructor and she said it was definitely illegal'. In the US, the AAA (American Automobile Association) at one point got so fed up with answering the question about footwear that they added a section called 'Barefoot Driving' to their annual *Digest of Motor Laws* to make it clear that 'Operation of a motor vehicle by a driver with bare feet is permitted.'

Public officials and road safety experts in the US, UK, Ireland, Canada, Australia, New Zealand and South Africa have all confirmed the same thing: it's a complete myth (at both federal and state levels where applicable). By way of a disclaimer: there *may* be a country somewhere on the planet that bans driving in bare feet, so you are reminded that a survey of all legislation in the world was not possible. (In Saudi Arabia it's illegal for women to drive, so you could technically argue that 'it's illegal for women to drive in bare

feet'.) However, in the countries listed, you can happily take your shoes and socks off if you don't mind the occasional verruca.

It's not entirely clear why there would be a law against driving in bare feet. If the concern is that it may be less safe than driving with shoes, which might depend on the type of shoes being compared, then you might ask why there is no law against driving while wearing boxing gloves (honestly, there isn't) and no law against driving with chewing gum stuck to your soles (again, there isn't, except perhaps in Singapore -- see p. 144). Due to the rather more exposed nature of motorcycles, many countries are rather firmer on the need for appropriate footwear if you're riding a motorbike. For cars, though, in all jurisdictions the advice from government officials is pretty much uniform: there's no law against driving with bare feet, but there are laws against the careless or dangerous operation of vehicles, and if the fact that you were driving with bare feet was a factor in the cause of any accident, this may have a bearing on the extent of your culpability.

## VERDICT: FALSE

In 2004 a government-funded road safety advert caused controversy in Australia's Northern Territory by showing a 'smart driver' hitting the brakes with his bare foot.

## It's illegal in the UK to shake a collection tin in the street, but no one ever does anything about it

THE TIME-HONOURED VIEW of the archetypal charity collector is that of a genteel old lady, standing stoically on the high street, shaking her collection tin to draw attention to her cause, with kindly members of the public occasionally stopping to doff their hats and part with a few low-denomination coins. Nowadays, however, this idyllic image has been viciously trampled to death by the Machiavellian corporate fundraising techniques adopted by charities that fight tooth and nail for their share of the public's cash. Charities are now concerned with outsourcing, return on investment, direct marketing, fundraising interactions, tax-effective giving and donor development.

One of the most visible effects of modern approaches to fundraising is the rise of 'face-to-face fundraising' – the successor to the genteel old lady. While charities call it 'face-to-face', rather more cynical members of the public have come to refer to it as 'chugging', or 'charity mugging', whereby hungover students and unemployed actors harangue you relentlessly in the street – even if you walk past them at the same location in your lunch hour *every single day* – pestering you vociferously to part not with your coins but with your bank details, in order to set up a Direct Debit. According to the UK's Public Fundraising Regulatory Association, charity giving has declined in the last 20 years, which explains why face-to-face has been increasingly used as a very effective tool. Although many people may be wary of handing over their bank details to surly, profit-motivated chuggers who know – and care – nothing about the causes they are promoting, the Direct Debit system actually contains sensible safeguards against fraud which mean it's a better approach than just handing over a one-off donation of cash; and of course chuggees are committing to regular payments, which allows charities to plan ahead more effectively. The only problem with the chuggers is that *they won't leave you alone*.

So with only Direct Debit forms to rustle, the whole tin-shaking issue isn't particularly relevant. But if you did want to go down the old-skool route, why on earth would shaking a collection tin be illegal? Some say that by shaking a tin you are technically 'begging'. Others claim that the shaking sound constitutes noise pollution, or even harassment.

Sadly, nothing so specific is enshrined in law. There is plenty of legislation covering street collections, including the delightfully vague Police, Factories, Etc. (Miscellaneous Provisions) Act 1916, which allows for local authorities to make their own regulations about where and when street collections can take place. Basically, you need to apply for a permit. More specifically, the Charitable Collections (Transitional Provisions) Order 1974 contains some very detailed instructions about carrying out collections, many of which relate to the sealing of collection boxes and the auditing and reporting of collected monies, in order to prevent fraudulent activity. The 1974 Order states that you have to be 25 metres away from any other collector and that you have to remain stationary; and if you tried to bust someone for not 'remaining stationary' on the basis that they were shaking their tin, you'd certainly get done for wasting police time. The legislation also clearly dictates that collections shall not be made 'in a manner likely to inconvenience or annoy any person' – so if you find tin-shaking annoying, you could try to get their permit revoked. Again, wasting police time seems to be the order of the day here.

When it comes to chuggers, they can carefully point out that this legislation refers only to the collection of cash or the sale of items for charity, and not to the collection of bank details. More recent legislation, such as the Charities Act 2006, was designed with modern considerations in mind, but there are still no specific regulations against tin-shaking.

## VERDICT: FALSE

In the spirit of the word 'chugger', someone has also probably coined the term 'churglar' – 'charity burglar' – to describe door-to-door fundraisers.

## In Sudan you can be forced to marry a goat

THIS DOESN'T SOUND VERY FAIR, does it? One minute you're wandering around minding your own business, and the next minute some meddling official forces you to enter into a lifelong union with a goat. Unless you're Zed out of *Police Academy* (see p. 63) it's not a very enticing prospect. However, the circumstances that led to a Sudanese man being forced to marry a goat were in fact motivated by a notion, no matter how questionable, of fairness.

In February 2006 Charles Tombe, from South Sudan, was caught in the act of having sex with a goat by the animal's owner, who promptly hauled him in front of local elders. Rather than recommending police action, the elders ordered Tombe to marry the goat and to pay the owner a dowry of 15,000 Sudanese dinars (roughly £35 or US$70). Not only did Charles Tombe – who didn't say much about the incident except that he was drunk at the time – get to keep the goat, but he also got to keep the goat's male offspring (not believed to be the result of their union). None of which seems particularly fair on the goat, called Rose, who died in May 2007.

The sad story of Tombe and his wife first appeared in the *Juba Post*, a weekly newspaper whose stated aims are 'to facilitate the development of civil society, to monitor good governance, to promote justice and to encourage South–South dialogue on peace and reconciliation'. (Perhaps a story about a bloke having sex with a goat comes under the 'development of civil society' part of the newspaper's remit, as an example to readers of 'what not to do'.) However, it gained international recognition after it was reported on the website of BBC News, an organisation who later expressed astonishment at how popular the item was: within a year the story had received 'several million hits', boosted by readers e-mailing the link around the world to bored friends and colleagues.

## VERDICT: TRUE

In December 2005 British tourist Sharon Tendler married a bottle-nose dolphin she had been visiting in Eilat, Israel, for many years; despite the misleading name of Cinderella, or Cindy for short, the dolphin was in fact male.


# Legally, Jaffa Cakes are biscuits

IF YOU LIVE IN THE UK, you'll be very familiar with the ever-popular Jaffa Cakes: chocolate-covered biscuits with the 'smashing orangey bit' in the middle. Well, you'd probably assume they're biscuits, despite their name, since you'll find boxes of McVitie's Jaffa Cakes in the biscuits aisle, alongside Rich Tea, Garibaldi, Digestives and the like. But as to whether they are 'legally' biscuits, who cares? It's not as if you'd ever find lawyers arguing in a courtroom about something so petty.

Or would you? In 1991 the UK tax authorities, in the form of the Commissioners of Customs and Excise, told McVitie's that Jaffa Cakes were biscuits. Somewhat randomly, it might seem, both biscuits and cakes are 'zero-rated' products under the Value Added Tax Act 1983, which means they are not taxable – but biscuits *are* subject to value-added tax at 17.5 per cent *if* they are covered in chocolate or chocolate substitute. McVitie's were firmly of the opinion that, as the product's name suggested, a Jaffa Cake is a cake, and that they should not be stumping up any cash, so their owners (the rather unfavourably named United Biscuits) appealed.

The London VAT Tribunal hearing quickly descended into a deep philosophical debate surrounding the nature of cakes and biscuits. The tribunal found that it was not a question of whether a Jaffa Cake was a cake or a biscuit, but more generally whether it was 'cake or non-cake'. Mr D.C. Potter QC (who described Jaffa Cakes' packaging as 'uncakelike') proceeded to the mind-blowing assertion that 'a product which is a biscuit (whether or not covered in chocolate) is capable of being also a cake'. At which point, we might all stop to consider whether a biscuit can be capable of 'being capable'.

Eventually Mr Potter ruled, once and for all, that Jaffa Cakes are 'cakes' – and furthermore, to avoid any future confusion, that Jaffa Cakes are also 'not biscuits'.

During the hearing, reference was made to a similar appeal in 1989 by Marks and Spencer, concerning their Caramel Shortcake Slices. On that occasion, Marks and Spencer submitted various food products to help their case, including exhibit A2: a box of six Harvest Currant Slices, exhibit A4: a box of Jaffa Cakes and exhibit A7: a box of six Mr Kipling Caramel Shortcakes. Customs & Excise upped the ante, by unveiling a rival selection of snacks, including their own box of Jaffa Cakes, a box of eight chocolate and black cherry biscuits, and – in a dazzling legal manoeuvre – a box of chocolate and orange thins. There followed a protracted discussion involving the similarities of shortcake and shortbread, although no one properly addressed the issue of whether shortbread is bread, or questioned how something could be 'a thin'. Eventually Marks and Spencer won their appeal, but not as a result of the tribunal panel bothering to define the technical characteristics, composition or preparation of a cake. No, the decisive factor of the panel was that 'in the unanimous view of the tribunal it tasted like a cake'.

**VERDICT: FALSE**

It would be nice to think that the victorious Marks and Spencer were awarded the right to scoff all the remaining exhibits.

## Technically, you should pay someone royalties for singing 'Happy Birthday to You'

EVEN IN COUNTRIES where English is not spoken, the singing of 'Happy Birthday to You' has become a standard for birthdays of any age, and is either a sweet reminder of being the centre of attention as a child, or a grating example of enforced entertainment. Whether you find it annoying or amusing, or even if you couldn't care less either way, you might be surprised to find that the song is still protected by copyright, after an extremely, extremely tortuous history. You have been warned.

In 1893 Mildred J. Hill was a musician and teacher at Louisville Experimental Kindergarten School in Kentucky, where her sister Patty Smith Hill was the principal. Together they wrote a song called 'Good Morning to All', which was published in a collection called *Song Stories for the Kindergarten*. The melody for 'Good Morning to All', credited to Mildred Hill, sounds the same as what we know today as 'Happy Birthday to You', but had the following lyrics, credited to her sister:

Good morning to you
Good morning to you
Good morning, dear children
Good morning to all.

(That's right, none of this new-fangled rhyming nonsense some songwriters go for: Patty obviously decided it would be better to end with the word 'all', although this was later replaced with another repetition of 'you', leading the song to become known thereafter as 'Good Morning to You'.) The only musical difference between the two versions is the rhythmic allowance for the two-syllable word 'happy' in place of the one-syllable word 'good', but this is not sufficient for anyone to successfully argue that they are two different pieces of music.

Patty Hill died in 1946, thirty years after her sister. Current copyright rules in the US and the European Union stipulate that copyright normally expires seventy years after an author or composer's death, which in Patty Hill's case would mean 2016. However, US copyright law hasn't always been so sensible, and for historical reasons, anything published prior to 1923 is in the public domain. Therefore there is no doubt that 'Good Morning to All' is out of copyright in terms of both its music and its lyrics.

So what about 'Happy Birthday to You'? Clearly, if the melody is the same then the only copyright that could still be in force relates to the words. Unfortunately, no one is quite certain who first came up with the birthday lyrics – and whoever it was, they failed to print a version of the text with a copyright notice, a practice that was a legal requirement for ensuring protection at the time (unlike modern-day copyright laws, in which copyright is automatically assigned). However, by the 1920s someone called Robert Coleman had begun publishing versions of the song that retained the 'Good Morning to You' words but added a second verse, comprising the 'Happy Birthday to You' lyrics. The popularity of this version quickly outshadowed the original.

In 1933 Jessica Hill, the sister of Patty and the late Mildred, was enraged to discover that the Broadway musical *As Thousands Cheer* featured 'Happy Birthday to You' alongside original works by Irving Berlin, and promptly set about suing the producers. (In fact, the song had already appeared on Broadway in the 1931 musical *The Band Wagon*.) Jessica Hill was not, of course, the original copyright holder, but it's safe to assume that she had a financial interest following her sister's death, in addition to a moral point to make on behalf of both her sisters. The court action led to the song being removed from *As Thousands Cheer*. The Hill family then authorised the Clayton F. Summy Company to publish and copyright 'Happy Birthday to You' in 1935, in an arrangement by Preston Ware Orem.

Under the 1909 Copyright Act then in force, copyright lasted 28 years from the date of publication, renewable for a further 28 years, so the owners duly extended the period in 1963. This would have meant copyright expiry in 1991 – but the 1976 Copyright Act retrospectively ensured that copyright was in force for 75 years from the date of first publication, meaning copyright expiry for 'Happy Birthday to You' in 2010. Yet again, however, US copyright law changed, under the 1998 Sonny Bono Copyright

Term Extension Act (no, really), extending existing copyright by a further 20 years.

In 1988 Warner/Chappell Music, then part of Warner Communications, bought what had once been the Clayton F. Summy Company, now Summy-Birchard, making them the current copyright owners.

You can of course sing 'Happy Birthday to You' privately without fear of litigation, but if you perform it publicly or record a version of it for distribution as a single, on an album or as a digital download, or if you include the song in a film or TV programme, you should be paying for it. In the case of the Mike Nichols-directed Broadway play *The Gin Game*, the producers had to pay a flat $25 per performance – which would have earned a total of $12,925 during the course of its 517-show run in 1977–8 (although the copyright owners didn't find out about it straight away). Warner/Chappell Music are rumoured to charge anything between $10,000 and $65,000 for use of the song in a movie, and are believed to earn between $1 million and $2 million annually in 'Happy Birthday' royalties. According to a *Time* magazine article written shortly before Warner/Chappell Music's acquisition of the rights, even Casio were paying a royalty of one cent for every digital watch programmed to play the song.

Before you feel too much sympathy for the Hill sisters' lack of financial remuneration, it has been suggested by many musicologists that songs such as 'Happy Greetings to All' and 'Good Night to You All', both in existence before 1893, may indicate that 'Good Morning to All' was itself ripped off other composers' work. We'll never know for sure.

Original or not, do Warner/Chappell Music actually have a

solid claim? Because the 1909 Copyright Act required notice of copyright to be published along with the work, and because versions prior to 1935 were published by Coleman and others without copyright notices, you could possibly argue that by 1935 the 'Happy Birthday to You' lyrics were already in the public domain. If you fancy a challenge, bring out a film called *Happy Birthday to You*, featuring numerous different cover versions of the song, wait for lawyers from Warner/Chappell Music to come knocking on your door, and see if they want to take it to court and risk having to pay back all that small change to Casio.

## VERDICT: TRUE, BUT IT'D BE WORTH TESTING IN COURT

Given that the last word of the third line of 'Happy Birthday to You' is effectively a blank – in other words, you fill in the gap with something like 'Aunt Patricia' or 'Mr President' – you could further attempt to argue that your version consists of original lyrics. Hey, Warner/Chappell Music, come and have a go if you think you're hard enough!

# In England you can get done for 'furious driving'

PICTURE THIS EVERYDAY SCENE. You're in the car on the way home, minding your own business, at the end of a perfect day. Suddenly, for no reason at all, the worst song you can possibly imagine comes on the radio. For the sake of argument, let's assume it's 'Lady in Red' by Chris de Burgh (who once claimed that Diana, Princess of Wales, told him she thought he'd written the song about her). Understandably, you're furious. Absolutely furious. However, you wisely decide not to try changing radio stations in case you cause a five-car pile-up, because that would probably earn you a conviction for 'dangerous driving'. So you continue driving furiously until the end of the sick-inducing musical horror. If an eagle-eyed police officer sees how furious you are, could you be fined for 'furious driving'?

If you're a London black cab driver, then yes you could. That's because there's a piece of legislation kicking around from the nineteenth century (the London Hackney Carriages Act 1843) that is still in force today, specifying a fine for licensed taxi drivers found guilty of 'wanton or furious driving' – the penalty for which is currently £200.

This obviously doesn't have any bearing on other motorists, so in this scenario, you're in the clear. However, what if you then saw Chris de Burgh himself standing in the middle of the road? High on emotion, you drive straight towards the man on the line. Timing is everything, and while de Burgh avoids making a fatal hesitation and uses his best moves to make the getaway, you still successfully run over his foot. In this case, you certainly won't be enjoying the ecstasy of flight down the road to freedom because the simple truth is that you could get prosecuted under the Offences Against the Person Act 1861, for causing 'any bodily harm to any person whatsoever' (which includes Chris de Burgh) 'by wanton or furious driving or racing'. Originally this was punishable by up to two years' imprisonment with hard labour.

English legislation relating to 'furious driving' dates back to the 1790s, when horse-drawn stage coaches could get out of hand, but even today motorists and cyclists are occasionally convicted for causing injury by 'wanton or furious driving' under the 1861 statute. Unfortunately, much-needed legislation banning Chris de Burgh has still not materialised.

**VERDICT: TRUE**
The offence of 'reckless driving' was re-branded as 'dangerous driving' in the Road Traffic Act 1991.

## The police recruit extra staff when it's a full moon

FOR CENTURIES HUMAN BEINGS have regarded the full moon as a time of many weird happenings: men transform into lycan-thropes, aggression is in the air, E.T. makes bicycles fly and people go mad. The word 'lunatic' and its abbreviation 'looney', whose origins in English can be traced back to the thirteenth century, derive from *luna*, the Latin for 'moon', because of the supposed associations between insanity and the monthly appearance of the earth's only natural satellite. Nowadays, of course, what with all that Renaissance and Enlightenment business a few centuries back, people don't believe this stuff, since it's a bunch of superstitious nonsense. But wait – if you look in most newspapers nowadays, you'll probably find a horoscope, purporting to link the movements of the stars and the planets with some vague blather about what will happen to you (yes, you, not the thousands of other readers) over the coming days and months.

Evidently superstitious beliefs persist, despite the unscientific and arbitrary nature of the horoscope: an article on astrology.com, for example, confidently asserts that Pluto 'governs crime and the underworld' and 'knows how to push buttons'. Pluto was only discovered in 1930, and in 2006 the International Astronomical Union stripped it of its planetary status. Yet astrologers are convinced it holds some ancient bearing over your life.

So for many people, the hardest scientific evidence won't be enough to convince them that celestial bodies don't hold some mysterious power over human beings (and werewolves). In the case of the 'full moon effect', rather a lot of research has been carried out.

Overwhelmingly, this research indicates that there is no reliable connection between the full moon and increased crime levels – but

there are some intriguing blips. For example, a company called Essex Medical & Forensic Services, who provide medical cover for a number of British police forces, 'revealed' in 2005 that the use of some new software from Microsoft enabled them to see that the peak times when medics were required were Friday and Saturday nights as well as 'at the full moon'. The absence of any actual data should in no way be interpreted as an attempt to grab headlines about the release of some new software from Microsoft.

When it comes to doctors – who might be on the receiving end of 'lunacy' – studies have looked at the incidence of admissions a few days after the full moon, and the results again strongly indicate that there is no link. A 1997 study carried out by Royal Liverpool University Hospital in the UK, published in the *International Journal of Social Psychiatry*, found no statistically significant 'lunar effects' on patients consulting their practitioners on matters of anxiety or depression. Nevertheless, there was a correlation (but not necessarily a causation) between the full moon and patients visiting general practitioners, according to a study by researchers from the University of Leeds published in 2000 in the journal *Family Practice* (idea for a sitcom: a husband and wife, their son and their daughter all end up as doctors in the same surgery, with hilarious consequences). They found a 'real, if small' rise in the number of consultations six days after a full moon.

Just in case you thought too much money was already being wasted on investigating this dubious area, there have been numerous 'studies of studies', in which researchers go back and analyse lots of previous studies to see whether there is any collective trend. One such 'meta-analysis', reported in the American Psychological Association's *Psychological Bulletin* in

1985, looked at 37 prior studies into links between the lunar cycle and numerous behavioural indicators, including hospital admissions and criminal offences. The finding was that the supposed phenomenon was unfounded, with any contrary conclusions in the earlier studies being due to 'inappropriate analyses, a failure to take other cycles into account, and a willingness to accept any departure from chance as evidence of a lunar effect'. Taking the whole 'studying other studies' concept to the extreme, consider professor Ivan W. Kelly of the University of Saskatchewan, who co-authored that 1985 study. According to National Geographic News, by 2004 Dr Kelly had published 15 papers on the 'full moon effect' and reviewed more than 50 others – including one that itself covered 200 previous studies. This guy has studied studies about studies and so he should know: according to Dr Kelly, the case for the full moon effect 'has not been made'.

Those who genuinely do believe that the lunar cycle – and not just the full moon specifically – has some sort of effect on human behaviour tend to put it down to the direct effects of gravitational pull (before you scoff, think about the oceans' tides, although admittedly oceans are rather more massive than humans) and the indirect effects of gravitational pull (changes in the tides trigger changes in ozone levels in the air). Let's be realistic, though: if hundreds of studies have been inconclusive and mostly find that there is no such effect, it's a pretty safe bet that any effect is negligible.

There could of course be rather more straightforward reasons why the full moon should lead to increased criminal activity. Put simply, if cloud cover is low then the full moon will create a brighter night-time – which could be a boon for muggers and burglars. However, while this could have a small effect on un-premeditated opportunism, anyone actually planning a burglary in this day and age would probably rely on something slightly more high-tech than the moon for light. But the light from the full moon can also simply mean more outdoor partying, with people staying out later and drinking more, leading to more public order incidents on the way back via the kebab shop.

So much for the theory. But *do* police forces actually institute any policy of additional staffing levels around the full moon? Unless there is a specific event organised around the phenomenon, police forces do not plan their staffing levels around the phases of the moon. As Australia's New South Wales Police put it: 'We prefer to stick with statistics, workload and computerised rostering to determine staffing levels.' The Royal Canadian Mounted Police note that the Inuit population in Labrador are particularly sensitive about the full moon, but that no changes in crime levels are observed – and there is no corresponding increase in staffing levels. It's the same story everywhere: the police do *not* recruit extra staff simply because the moon is out.

Except, that is, in the English city of Brighton and Hove, where in June 2007 Sussex Police flew in the face of science by announcing that they would deploy additional officers, after their own research suggested 'a general positive correlation' between violent incidents and the full moon. Inspector Andy Parr, who led the research, 'explained' that the moon 'has a strong influence on tides, and magnetic forces can influence people's psyche' – and added that he would be 'interested in approaching the universities and seeing if any of their postgraduates would be interested in looking into it further'. Perhaps he should just consult Dr Ivan W. Kelly.

## VERDICT: ONLY IN EAST SUSSEX

One proven effect of the lunar cycle is that anyone who's watched *An American Werewolf in London* will instinctively find themselves saying 'Beware the moon, lads' every time it's a full moon.

# Chewing gum is a controlled substance in Singapore

IT'S KIND OF ANNOYING, isn't it, when you're on a Tube train and grasp the handrail, only to have your fingers close on a revolting old piece of gum stuck to the underside. In such moments, it would be great if you could just outlaw chewing gum altogether. In 1992 that's exactly what Singapore did, partly due to the authorities' general annoyance at the cleaning costs and partly due to specific concerns around chewing gum interfering with automatic sensors on the train doors of the city's Mass Rapid Transit system (which apparently only has one station – see p. 239).

An outright ban remained in place for twelve years, and affected 'the substance usually known as chewing gum, bubble gum or dental chewing gum, or any like substance prepared from a gum base of vegetable or synthetic origin and intended for' – you guessed it – 'chewing'. Technically, the actual chewing of gum was not subject to any legal restrictions, probably because of the impracticality of being able to recruit enough mouth police to do all the checking. Instead, various pieces of legislation prohibited the manufacture, sale and importation of gum, such as the Control of Manufacture Act, the rather specific Sale of Food (Prohibition of Chewing Gum) Regulations, and the somewhat tautological Regulation of Imports and Exports (Chewing Gum) Regulations. These were backed up by some pretty tough fines for littering.

In 2004 the rules were relaxed slightly, to allow the importation and regulated sale of chewing gum 'intended for use in promoting dental health or oral hygiene'. Under the new system, an establishment may be granted a licence under the Medicines Act to offer gum for sale by prescription, if that gum has proven health benefits; but if you don't have such a licence then you can be fined up to S$2,000 (in the region of £700 or US$1,300) for selling or advertising chewing gum.

**VERDICT: TRUE**
The Singaporean authorities didn't change the rules out of a burning desire to increase the country's dental health: the amendments were conceded as part of negotiations relating to a free trade agreement with the US, driven by demands on behalf of Wrigley from then-Congressman Phil Crane.

## It's illegal for a pub to serve snakebite

IN THE UK, where binge-drinking is a national sport, it's a matter of patriotic pride that snakebite can be claimed as a British invention. (The drink, together with its associated 'lifestyle concept', has since been successfully exported to Australia and elsewhere.) Should you not have had the pleasure of experiencing this alcoholic 'treat', you may be interested to learn a bit about its composition – which may go some way to explaining its allegedly outlawed status.

Your basic, entry-level snakebite consists of half a pint of lager and half a pint of cider, mixed together in a pint glass – to form a drink which seems to have an intoxicating effect greater than the sum, or even the multiplication, of its parts. (A note to American readers: we're talking 'hard cider' here, so not a splash of beer topped up with some cloudy apple juice.) But many drinkers – who tend to be students seeking the most cost-effective way of getting wasted – choose any of several more elaborate variations, partly because, in its simplest form, snakebite tastes pretty horrible. You could try a snakebite 'n' black, sometimes referred to as a Purple Nasty or Diesel, which uses a shot of blackcurrant cordial to disguise the underlying taste. Or, if you want to go for some serious power-drinking, you can ramp up the core ingredients to a super-strength lager (Special Brew or Tennent's Super – take your pick) and an industrial-grade cider. Finally, as the *pièce de résistance*, you could add a 'depth charge': a shot of Pernod, peach schnapps or some other suitably sickly spirit, dropped (glass and all) into the pint.

The effects of such an abhorrent mix of alcoholic beverages are fairly predictable, causing many a drinker quickly to lose the ability to speak coherently and, more seriously, increase their likelihood of challenging anyone or anything to settle any matter with an ill-coordinated attempt at a fight. It's probably this reputation that leads landlords routinely to refuse to serve snakebite, rather than the fact that it is illegal as such, and plenty of pubs and bars in the UK (not least those in student unions) will happily serve you a pint of the stuff, if not a pitcher. On the other hand, you'll also come across the occasional barman who will knowingly serve you a half of lager and a half of cider in two separate glasses (one of which is a pint glass), turning a blind eye to the fact that you want to mix your own snakebite – which seems to lend credence to the 'it's technically illegal' theory.

For all the talk, you won't be too surprised to learn that there is nothing approaching a 'Serving of Snakebite (Prohibition of) Act' in the laws of England, Wales or Scotland, and in fact any legislation relating to the mixing of alcohol is concerned with the payment of excise duty, which wouldn't really be relevant by the time a landlord might choose to serve you a pint of snakebite. In any case, there would be no particular reason to single out the snakebite from any other mixed drink now existing or hereafter invented. Pubs that refuse to serve it do so as a management policy, to deter the types of behaviour and reputation associated with the drink's real or perceived effects – and some probably claim 'it's the law' to minimise the risk of drunk patrons trying to argue the case.

## VERDICT: FALSE

In 2001 Bill Clinton was politely refused a request for a pint of snakebite to accompany a steak and ale pie in the Old Bell Tavern in Harrogate, North Yorkshire; the establishment eventually served the former US president a Coke, although he tasted a couple of real ales before deciding on the opposite end of the alcoholic spectrum.

# P. Diddy was sued for trading under the name of Diddy in the UK

SEAN JOHN COMBS REGARDS HIMSELF as some kind of latter-day Renaissance man, with his finger in every pie of the entertainment world: he is or has been a record producer, hip-hop performer, head of Bad Boy Records, fashion designer, movie star and Arsenal fan. Indeed, according to his official biography, by the end of 2006 he had 'upped his moguldom to unprecedented levels, adding fragrance producer, Broadway actor, marathon runner, and television producer to his growing list of accomplishments'. Upping our moguldom is something many of us can only dream about. In Sean Combs' case it has made him one of the richest figures in showbiz, and if any further evidence of his moguldom-upping were required, he has two annual 'Diddy Days' in his honour: 14 May in Las Vegas and 13 October in Chicago – although check back in five years' time to see if anyone is still marking the occasion.

Obviously if you have any involvement in hip-hop, it's very 'un-street' to go by your own name, so it's customary to adopt one or more stage names that establish your credentials as someone to be taken seriously in a world dominated by images of guns and gangstas. Unfortunately, Sean Combs has had trouble with the 'being taken seriously' part by adopting names like Puff Daddy and P. Diddy. However, he has managed to compensate for this by being accused of shadowy involvement in the circumstances surrounding the shootings of Tupac Shakur and the Notorious B.I.G., and he seems to be constantly implicated in one court case after another, whether it's assault, reckless driving, weapons offences or health and safety breaches.

One such court case was threatened in late 2005 after he publicly announced that he was shortening his name from P. Diddy to Diddy. He explained at the time that people weren't sure what to call him, and he had specific problems on the phone: 'When I'd called someone on the telephone it took me a long time to explain who I was. Too long.' Dropping the 'P.' would have saved him at least half a second per call, but it also landed him in court for trademark infringement.

First in the queue for suing were not, as you might expect, British 'comedian' Ken Dodd's Diddy Men, or even Burger King (for ripping off their whole Diddy Donuts concept), or Donkey Kong's sidekick Diddy Kong (who is actually a monkey, unlike Donkey Kong – see p. 68). His diddy nemesis turned out to be a British DJ who also has a name that no one can take seriously: Richard 'Diddy' Dearlove, who had been putting out music in the UK under the 'Diddy' name since 1992. It should also be noted that the British DJ Richard 'Diddy' Dearlove can't be sued by the British DJ 'Diddy' David Hamilton, because the latter was given his nickname when working with Ken Dodd, who had every right to assign the 'Diddy' moniker to those worthy of it.

Under the terms of an initial agreement reached in September 2006, Sean Combs paid Richard Dearlove £10,001 plus significant costs and agreed to redirect www.diddyonline.com to www.p-diddy.co.uk for UK visitors to his site, as well as ensuring that records and other merchandise sold in the UK identified him as P. Diddy or another name, but not just Diddy. Unfortunately in February 2007 P. Diddy was found to be in breach of the agreement, partly because of material appearing on third-party websites, and partly because of a lyric appearing on his October 2006 *Press Play* album, 'mainline this new Diddy heroin' – which P. Diddy agreed to remove from British performances of his song 'The Future' in, er, the future.

In the initial hearing, Mr Justice Kitchin found that the extent of P. Diddy's control over the third-party website content was difficult to ascertain, and rather than imposing an injunction, ordered that the case go to full trial, unless an out-of-court settlement could subsequently be reached. In the meantime, the public at large can chuckle at the fact that Mr Justice Kitchin had to express his thoughts concerning whether lyrics such as 'Diddy got it wrapped like cocoons, Pop shit like needles through balloons' constituted 'advertisement within the UK of goods and services'. If you're a student of the law and want an entertaining read, look up *Dearlove (trading and professionally known as 'Diddy') v Combs (trading and professionally known as 'Sean "Puffy" Combs', 'Puffy' and 'P. Diddy')*.

## VERDICT: TRUE

P. Diddy has had to publicly deny suffering from coulrophobia – the fear of clowns – amid rumours that he demands a 'no-clowns' clause in his touring contracts.

### In England, if you don't pay your water bill, legally they can't cut you off

IT'S GENERALLY ACCEPTED that if you don't pay the bill for services or goods already received, you probably won't be very welcome next time you come to make a purchase. But pub lawyers will assure you that you can run up as high a water bill as you like without any fear of your supply being cut.

When it comes to gas and electricity, it's very clear: no money, no supply. The utility companies will of course take reasonable means to avoid disconnecting you, so if you're late in paying for only a short time or if you agree to repay in instalments, they won't be particularly trigger-happy. But basically, it's wise not to mess with them.

Water, on the other hand, is a different story. The various water companies in England, such as Northumbrian Water, Thames Water, Anglian Water and Yorkshire Water, all issue advice to consumers on 'what to do if you're having difficulty paying your bill'. As you'd expect, the general theme of such guidelines is the common-sense approach that you should let them know sooner rather than later that you're having financial problems, so that they can work out a sensible compromise. Many water regions, such as Severn Trent, have associated Charitable Trust Funds that can provide financial assistance to those in exceptional circumstances, while special tariffs for 'vulnerable groups' are sometimes available too. But when you dig into the detail of what the water companies threaten to do in the case of non-payment, you won't be surprised to learn that their leaflets do not feature

prominent headlines such as 'Use as much water as you want! We can't legally cut you off!'

The legislation in question is the Water Industry Act 1991 (as amended in 1999), which explicitly prohibits water companies from disconnecting supplies due to non-payment. The rules apply to certain categories of customer, including domestic premises, hospitals, nursing homes, schools, prisons, police stations, and, er, house-boats (can't they just siphon water out of the canal?). If you're a business, however, you can be disconnected.

So what if you don't pay? The water company will take you to court, following which they have a range of options: getting a court order to deduct funds directly from your income, sending in the bailiffs (with or without baseball bats) to take your possessions, getting a garnishee order (which sounds like a side-salad but enables them to raid your bank account) and initiating bankruptcy proceedings. In short, it probably wouldn't be much fun.

If you're merrily running up a massive water bill in England and you think it might be a good idea to skip the country, bear in mind that things aren't quite so lenient everywhere else. A traditional destination for English criminals on the run is Spain: in that country, you can probably get away with not paying your bill for about a year, but after that they *will* cut you off. Just to make sure you get the message, they'll also charge you a reconnection fee.

## VERDICT: TRUE
Northumbrian Water's headquarters are in the intriguingly named town of Pity Me, County Durham.

# HISTORY

## Rudolph the Red-Nosed Reindeer was invented for a department store

THERE ARE MANY KILLJOYS OUT THERE who will insist that the modern-day, red-suited image of Santa Claus was cynically invented by money-driven, cheap-suited executives at The Coca-Cola Company. While the illustrations Haddon Sundblom created for Coke in the 1930s certainly helped to cement this vision of Santa as the 'traditional' Christmas image, Santa had existed in that form for many years.

But killjoys, take heart! Unlike Santa, his helper Rudolph really *is* the methodically manufactured result of a department store seeking proactively to synergise new customer-facing, go-to-market efficiencies by impactfully mind-sharing best-of-breed promotional solutions aimed at a sub-adult demographic.

The verse story of Rudolph was created in 1939 by copywriter Robert L. May, an employee of the Chicago-based Montgomery Ward retail chain. Montgomery Ward was started in 1872 as a mail-order business, then expanded into hundreds of stores during the twentieth century, before going spectacularly bankrupt at the

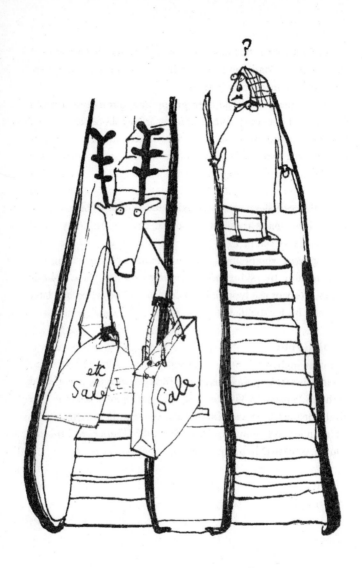

end of 2000, with the brand name being resuscitated a few years later by Direct Marketing Services Inc. for the purposes of a web-based and, er, mail-order business.

Montgomery Ward had been giving away promotional books for a number of years, before deciding that May should create their own publication in-house, as a way to save money. They distributed over two million copies of the first edition of his booklet; and given the long-term popularity of Rudolph, you'd think that by retaining the copyright in the story (since May was working as an employee of the company when he wrote it) Montgomery Ward would have made millions of dollars out of the shiny-nosed reindeer. However, in 1947 they generously transferred the copyright to May, who promptly began commercially exploiting it – most notably by asking his songwriter brother-in-law, Johnny Marks, to adapt the lyrics into a Christmas standard, which later became a hit for the likes of Gene Autry and Bing Crosby.

## VERDICT: TRUE

The first eight of Santa's reindeer – Dasher, Dancer, Prancer, Vixen, Comet, Cupid, Donner and Blitzen – originally appeared in the 1823 poem 'A Visit from St Nicholas', known today as 'The Night Before Christmas'; Donner and Blitzen, the German words for 'thunder' and 'lightning', were then called Dunder and Blixem (Dutch, or near-Dutch, equivalents).

## Adolf Hitler was *Time* magazine's
## Man of the Year in 1938

THE PROBLEM *Time* MAGAZINE has is convincing people that
their Person of the Year award, launched originally as Man of the
Year in 1927 (aviator Charles Lindbergh), is not intended as
recognition of a praiseworthy individual. Although they point out
that the award simply acknowledges the person who, in their
opinion, has had the most significant impact on world events over
the preceding 12 months, there will always be those who assume
that *Time* magazine implicitly endorses the views and
achievements of the selected individual.

So when people tell you that Hitler was *Time*'s Man of the Year
in 1938, which he was, they're trying to suggest that the great
American media institution actually supported Hitler in the
months leading up to the Second World War. This is, of course,
very wide of the mark. As stated in the accompanying cover story,
the key reason for his selection was that in 1938 he became 'the
greatest threatening force that the democratic, freedom-loving
world faces today'. The article contained the fascinating piece of
trivia that exactly 1,133 streets and squares had been renamed in
Hitler's honour, and concluded with the comment that 'the Man
of 1938 may make 1939 a year to be remembered.' Indeed.

While those who own *Time* magazine – part of the media
conglomerate that encompasses AOL, Warner Bros., HBO, the
Cartoon Network, New Line Cinema, CNN, and a lot more
besides – undoubtedly don't want to be thought of as supporting
the likes of Hitler and Stalin (who was chosen in both 1939 and

1942), they certainly love the publicity. Every December their choice of Person of the Year 'raises eyebrows' among commentators, columnists, talking heads, pundits and other people routinely paid to 'raise eyebrows'. More irritating than controversial is the occasional selection of a non-person, such as Endangered Earth (replacing the Person of the Year as Planet of the Year in 1988) and The Middle Americans (in 1969). In 2006 things became revoltingly 'knowing' when, to acknowledge the influence of what the eyebrow-raisers term 'Web 2.0' (blogging, Wikipedia, YouTube, MySpace – you know the routine), *Time* decided that Person of the Year was You. Pass the sick bag, please.

## VERDICT: TRUE, BUT SO WHAT?
The 1938 Man of the Year cover was an illustration by exiled Catholic Baron Rudolph Charles von Ripper showing, in *Time*'s words, 'Adolf Hitler playing his hymn of hate in a desecrated cathedral while victims dangle on a St. Catherine's wheel and the Nazi hierarchy looks on.'

# The White House used to be grey

YOU MAY HAVE ENCOUNTERED MANY an armchair historian who confidently claims that the President's official residence was originally painted grey (or *gray*, as an inhabitant of the building in question would spell it). If the historian is particularly diligent, the claim might then be backed up with the further detail that 1600 Pennsylvania Avenue was not painted white until after British troops set fire to it in 1814, with the paint being used to redecorate the repaired exterior and cover the burn marks and smoke damage.

The building certainly was gutted by fire during the War of 1812 – which, confusingly, didn't end until 1815 – as a result of the Brits being in a huff after the Americans burned down lots of their buildings in York (modern-day Toronto). The damage was so extensive that only the outer sandstone shell of the building survived; and once it had been fully repaired, they certainly did apply the whitewash – but not for the first time, because the building had been painted that colour during its original construction, which began in 1792 and ended some time after John 'not Quincy' Adams took up residence there in 1800.

The building was designed (without the modern-day North and South porticoes) by Irishman James Hoban, who is said to have taken as his inspiration Leinster House in Dublin – then the Duke of Leinster's residence and today the Irish parliament building. (Just to complicate matters, Leinster House was designed by a German, Richard Cassels.) The confusion about the original colour of Hoban's building was probably not due to the fact that Leinster House was (and is) grey, but rather the fact that the term 'White House' wasn't in widespread usage until shortly before the War of 1812, with the building being referred to previously as the President's House, the President's Palace or the Presidential Mansion.

## VERDICT: WHITEWASH

There is a one-lane bowling alley underneath the North Portico of the White House, built for the Nixons, who were massive bowling fans.

# You have to be dead to appear in the National Portrait Gallery

TOURISTS TO LONDON often miss the National Portrait Gallery, even though it's right next to the main National Gallery in Trafalgar Square. For those who are aware of its existence, when time is short and you're faced with the choice between 'pictures of lots of different things' and 'pictures of dead people', most people will probably go for the less specific option, unless they have a particular love of portraits, or of dead people. Because dead people it mostly is, based on selection criteria that relate not to the perceived artistic merit of the portraits, but to the historical importance of the subjects. Which means that if a four-year-old had scrawled a picture of Edward the Confessor on some toilet paper, the National Portrait Gallery would do their best to acquire it. Of course, a four-year-old attempting this 1,000 years later doesn't count, since the subject needs to have been drawn, painted or photographed from life. (Forgers take note: toilet paper had not been invented in the eleventh century.)

The gallery owes its existence to the perseverance of Philip Stanhope, the fifth Earl Stanhope, who finally managed to establish the gallery in 1856, at first in temporary premises. It moved to its present site in 1896, which gradually expanded during the twentieth century as new surrounding land became available. Stanhope's original vision was for portraits of 'those persons who are most honourably commemorated in British history as warriors or as statesmen, or in arts, in literature or in science'. More specifically, the gallery's original trustees declared a ten-year cut-off rule:

'No portrait of any person still living, or deceased less than 10 years, shall be admitted by purchase, donation, or bequest, except only in the case of the reigning Sovereign, and of his or her Consort.'

All that changed in 1968, when the gallery mounted an exhibition of photographs by Cecil Beaton, whose focus was very much modern-day celebrity, in contrast to the historical and august images with which the National Portrait Gallery had become associated. The following year, the decision was taken to permit portraits of living people into the gallery's collection on a permanent basis, and since 1992 the official policy has been to

acquire and maintain 'portraits in all media of the most eminent persons in British history from the earliest times to the present day', as well as collecting documents relating to portraiture and occasionally commissioning portraits.

As a result, Philip Stanhope would be enraged to discover that today's National Portrait Gallery owns portraits of such luminaries of British culture as Johnny Vaughan, Richard and Judy, Craig David, Ant and Dec, Dale Winton, Billie Piper, Tony Blackburn and Russ Abbot – although mercifully none of these are actually on public display. He'd probably also want to hear a fairly convincing argument as to why the gallery holds portraits of Martin Sheen, Björk, Lauren Bacall, Tina Turner and Steven Spielberg, who are not noted for their Britishness.

**VERDICT: FALSE**

In 2001, despite his many years advertising Hamlet cigars, Russ Abbot was declared Pipesmoker of the Year by the Pipesmokers' Council (who no longer hand out the annual award, following the 2002 Tobacco Advertising and Promotion Act); this must surely be the reason for his qualification as an 'eminent person'.

# London Underground nicked its logo from the YMCA

THE LONDON UNDERGROUND 'ROUNDEL' consists of a red circle with a cut-out centre, crossed by a horizontal blue band. Doesn't the YMCA logo – in the US, Canada and Australia at least – involve the black letter Y with a red triangle forming part of the letter? The UK's design is different – the word 'YMCA', in white letters, with a red triangle slotting into the top of the Y – but it still doesn't look anything like the iconic symbol of the transport system used by around three million passengers a day. There is a circular logo used by the World Alliance of YMCAs, with 'Asia', 'Europa', 'Oceania', 'Africa' and 'America' around the outside and some suitably Christian imagery in the centre – but you'd have to be Mr Magoo to mistake it for the entrance to a tube station.

Today's World Alliance logo was in fact the first standard logo agreed upon by the YMCA, in 1881. However, numerous designs have been used since, the most notable of which was Luther H. Gulick's creation of a red triangle with a cut-out centre in 1891. Apparently the shape – unofficial at first – represented the balance of spirit, mind and body, and the three words would often appear written on each side of the triangle. A couple of clumsy-looking hybrid logos then emerged, with the red triangle superimposed on the main part of the World Alliance logo. Some time around the First World War, however, a clean version of the triangle, without the World Alliance clutter, was created, onto which was placed a blue horizontal band, extending beyond the edges of the triangle, containing the word 'YMCA' in white letters. It's this red-white-and-blue, triangle-and-band device (used up until 1967, when the present-day 'Y' logo was adopted) that looks not dissimilar to the familiar London Underground logo. To be blunt, it looks like someone working for the Underground saw the YMCA logo and thought: 'Hey, let's take the triangle and change it into a circle; then, the clever bit is that we replace "YMCA" with the word "UNDERGROUND"!'

In fact, that's sort of what happened when Frank Pick (largely responsible for establishing the 'corporate identity' of what was to become London Transport) asked typographer Edward Johnston (who designed the typeface that is used to this day, largely unchanged, across the Underground) to develop a new 'bullseye' logo for the organisation. To be fair to Johnston, who completed the design in 1919, there was an existing bullseye device in use, which consisted of a solid circle with text across it, but he was certainly instructed to create something similar to the YMCA logo by Pick, who found it particularly striking.

**VERDICT: AHEM, 'INSPIRED BY', RATHER THAN 'NICKED'**
In 2004 Landor Associates unveiled a new design for the women's equivalent, the YWCA; they abolished a 1988 creation by legendary movie-titles designer Saul Bass and instead developed a logo containing *only text* – ooh, controversial!

# A bloke had hiccups for 68 years

MOST OF US SUFFER the occasional bout of hiccups – or hiccoughs, if you prefer the olde-worlde spelling – for a few minutes, during which time we find ourselves besieged with advice from friends about drinking out of the wrong side of the glass, breathing into a paper bag, eating gherkins or naming as many bald men as you can think of. Eventually you notice that they've simply gone away (the hiccups, not the bald men, who were probably never there to start with, unless your hiccups began while you were at a Bruce Willis lookalike competition).

For some people, however, it can take weeks, and in extreme cases years, for hiccups to subside, by which point the sufferer has probably named a million bald men. In these situations, quite aside from the annoyance factor, persistent hiccupping can cause medical problems such as pulling stomach muscles and tearing the oesophagal lining.

The medical term for hiccupping is singultus – doctors couldn't just call it 'hiccupping', could they? – and to this day no one really understands why it happens. The involuntary spasms of the diaphragm and the subsequent closures of the glottis seem to be caused by irritation to the phrenic and vagus nerves, and where medical intervention is really felt to be necessary, this tends to involve sedation, effectively switching the relevant bits of your brain off for a while, or if absolutely necessary, surgery to the phrenic or vagus nerves.

Cases measured in years are rare but not unheard of. In December 2000 a man called Bill Holloway from Covington, Virginia, finished a bowl of soup – Campbell's Chunky Soup, apparently – and was still hiccupping over six years later at the age of 84. John Francis Crosland, of Laurinburg, North Carolina, started hiccupping in 1961 and hadn't stopped in 2004, by which time he had bought a customised registration plate for his car, reading 'HICUPMAN'.

The longest case of hiccupping, however, was that of Charles Osborne of Iowa, who hiccupped continually for 68 years, starting in 1922 while he was slaughtering a pig. Osborne was in the process of hanging the pig from a tree branch when he shouted for his wife to help him – and at that moment the hiccups struck. (To set this story in context, it should be noted that Charles Osborne was a farmer, so it's not as if stringing pigs up on trees was some kind of weird pastime.) In 1988 he rather perceptively told a newspaper: 'Someday it's gonna kill me, I s'pose. Or else I'll just die.' In 1990 his hiccups finally stopped, spontaneously, and the following year he died of unrelated causes.

### VERDICT: TAKE A DEEP BREATH, HOLD IT FOR AS LONG AS YOU CAN, THEN BREATHE OUT SLOWLY... TRUE

In 2006 Francis M. Fesmire of the University of Tennessee College of Medicine and Majed Odeh, Harry Bassan and Arie Oliven of Israel's Bnai Zion Medical Center won Ig Nobel awards – handed out for achievements 'that first make people laugh, and then make them think' – for their medical case reports titled 'Termination of Intractable Hiccups with Digital Rectal Massage'. You probably wouldn't want to shake hands with them any time soon, though.

## Britain is still paying back debts from the Napoleonic Wars

IF YOU'RE PAYING OFF a mortgage on your house and then take a 'repayment holiday' because you're getting into financial difficulties (perhaps because you were recently made redundant, or because you want to blow six months' salary on pizzas and lottery scratchcards), you can be reasonably sure that if you quietly try to continue *not paying* for the next few decades, the bank will sit up and take notice. In fact, if you don't cough up the money when they send the guy with the baseball bat round, it won't be long before they repossess your house and you end up having to move in with your mother-in-law, which sounds like the premise for a drab 1970s sitcom (or a drab 2007 sitcom, judging by the Nicholas Lyndhurst vehicle *After You've Gone*).

When it comes to national governments lending each other money, it's an altogether different game. Frankly, you'd be amazed how relaxed countries can be about bothering to pay each other back. Take the Paris Club, for example: an 'informal group' of creditors representing 19 governments who discuss problems with countries' debt repayments. In the case of Nigeria, they agreed that the country could stump up $12.4 billion (which it succeeded in doing in 2006) in exchange for writing off the rest of Nigeria's $30 billion debts. The Paris Club also announced in 2007 that they would completely write off all the money owed to them by Sierra Leone – over $200 million. When you're talking these kinds of figures, that's what you want: an *informal group* of creditors, evoking images of ruddy-faced old men in dinner jackets sitting around in creaky armchairs, puffing on cigars and knocking back sherry before heading off to watch some hot can-can action (and deciding whether to restructure Zambia's external public debt in the taxi on the way there).

It's not just African nations that have problems paying off their loans. The United Kingdom has a particularly poor record when it comes to costs arising directly or indirectly from war. The British government borrowed over $4 billion from the United States following the end of the Second World War – and made the last of 50 payments only on 29 December 2006 (six years late). However, when it comes to the First World War, the UK sort of, ahem, stopped paying the US back in the 1930s, by which time the outstanding amount was already over $4 billion. And, you know, the Americans kind of never really asked Britain to sort

things out – not properly, anyway – and, well, you know how it is, it would have been more awkward to bring it up than ignore it. Technically if the British government were to honour the debt, they'd need to find a spare $80 billion in today's money.

Going further back in time, the Napoleonic Wars were an

expensive period for the Kingdom of Great Britain (which became the United Kingdom of Great Britain and Ireland with the 1800 Act of Union). Between 1793 and the defeat of Napoleon Bonaparte at Waterloo in 1815, Britain's national debt pretty much quadrupled and rose to something like 250 per cent of nominal GDP (a ratio not subsequently matched until the end of the Second World War). Much of the cash raised, and hence owed, took the form of consols. The consol – a shortened form of 'consolidated annuities' – was a concept dreamt up in the 1750s by Sir Henry Pelham, in his dual capacity as Prime Minister and Chancellor of the Exchequer, as an ingenious way to consolidate the government's wide and confusing range of outstanding debts into a unified 3.5 per cent bond, resulting in lower payments by the government. (For those who spend too much time watching adverts on daytime TV, this was an official way of Sir Henry Pelham enthusiastically telling the Treasury: 'Consolidate all your debts into one easy payment!') Thanks largely to some economic jiggery-pokery by Chancellor George Goschen in 1888, the consols' coupon rate (effectively the interest rate) was eventually reduced to 2.5 per cent, which is what it remains to this day, for the £200 million or so still in issue. With such a low interest rate, the reasoning is that continuing to pay out on the consols represents a better deal for the national debt than buying them back.

## VERDICT: TRUE

In 1945 the last American descendant of the Bonaparte family, Jerome-Napoleon Charles Bonaparte, fatally broke his neck in Central Park after tripping over the leash of his wife's dog.

# London used to have an Eastminster Abbey as well as a Westminster Abbey

YOU'VE HEARD OF WESTMINSTER ABBEY (if you haven't, you should probably be reading *The Very Hungry Caterpillar* instead): site of Poet's Corner, scene of many a royal wedding, and the final resting place of hundreds of latter-day celebrities such as Sir Isaac Newton, a guy called Joshua 'Spot' Ward (who apparently yanked George II's dodgy thumb back into place) and Henry V and his wife Catherine de Valois – whose embalmed body was kept on display for centuries and was kissed on the lips by the creepy Samuel Pepys in 1669, over 200 years after her death. You might not know that Westminster Abbey's official name is the Collegiate Church of St Peter, Westminster, but then no one cares because no one calls it that – just as no one cares that Big Ben is technically the nickname for the Great Bell of Westminster, and not the name of its tower at the Palace of Westminster (which is actually St Stephen's Tower, or simply The Clock Tower).

It's tempting to think that an Eastminster Abbey might be some sort of 'evil twin' of Westminster Abbey: lurking in an alleyway under the shadow of the Tower of London, dark and mysterious, and home to the tombs of ne'er-do-wells such as Jack the Ripper, Harold Shipman and Bob Hope. In fact, Eastminster Abbey was an alternative name (as was New Abbey) for St Mary Graces, or sometimes St Mary of the Graces, which was indeed situated near the Tower of London, in East Smithfield. The establishment was a Cistercian abbey founded around 1350 by Edward III, in gratitude to God for getting him through a particularly rough journey at sea.

According to John Stow's classic *Survey of London* (1598), after St Mary Graces had been demolished in the 1500s, it was replaced with a storehouse and 'convenient ovens' for the 'baking of biscuits to serve her majesty's ships'. You can only begin to imagine the disastrous consequences that would have ensued if the biscuit ovens had turned out to be somehow inconvenient.

The Royal Mint (which had previously been inside the Tower of London) was eventually built over part of the site of St Mary Graces in 1811, although in the 1960s it moved to Llantrisant in Wales, where all British coins are manufactured today.

### VERDICT: TRUE

During Richard II's reign St Mary Graces had a prior, William de Wendover, as well as an abbot, William de Warden; they probably frittered away the evenings arguing about the difference between an abbey and a priory, while each accused the other of nicking the idea for his name.

## Isaac Newton invented the cat flap

THERE ARE SO MANY STORIES about Isaac Newton that it's often impossible to determine which ones are true, which were made up by his detractors, and which were originally true but have become distorted over time. He certainly had a reputation for absent-mindedness – forgetting to eat, not remembering his own relatives' names, and so on – and the prevailing image is of someone who was a genius and yet lacked some fundamental 'life skills'.

Sadly, the origins of the story about the cat flap (also known as a 'cat door' or sometimes 'kitty door') are difficult to pin down. It has been suggested that the source was John Aubrey (who gave us the tale of Francis Bacon's demise – see p. 192). However, the only mention of Newton in his *Brief Lives* is the accusation that he ripped off Robert Hooke's ideas on gravity. The cat flap story has clearly been around for centuries, but its exact source is unclear. And the fact that there are so many different variants on the tale does make its likely accuracy somewhat suspect, to say the least. According to some versions, he simply cut a hole in the door of his barn to let his cat in and out. Others will have you believe that he was being disturbed by his cat scratching and mewing to be let in and out of his study while he was trying to concentrate on writing. Then again, it's also said that the cat was pushing open the door to his attic, letting in the light and spoiling his experiments on optics, so he created a hole covered by dark felt flaps. Finally it's been suggested that he cut the hole in the front door to his Lincolnshire home of Woolsthorpe Manor. However, if any such hole-in-the-door existed at Woolsthorpe Manor, it has long since been repaired, because there is no evidence for it today.

An entertaining addendum to the story is the suggestion that when the cat had kittens, Newton cut a separate smaller hole for them to use – in other words, he didn't work out that the smaller kittens could simply use the existing larger hole – much to the amusement of his contemporaries. But perhaps this is just another vicious rumour propagated by Newton-sceptics.

Newton's invention of the cat flap gets a mention in *Dirk Gently's Holistic Detective Agency* by Douglas Adams, as the kind of thing that seems so obvious you wonder why no one else invented it first. And it's quite possible that they did. Cats have of course been

domesticated for millennia – the ancient Egyptians revered them – but they're not stupid animals and so they would have come and gone via any openings in a building that they could fit through. So it seems likely that the need for a special way to let cats in and out of a house would only have arisen after the widespread use of glass in windows (something that became regular practice in England at the beginning of the seventeenth century, not long before Newton's birth) and the need for solid doors on houses (a phenomenon that had obviously become common long before his time).

While holes cut into house doors for cats seem to have been relatively common in the south of France in the mid-1700s, not long after Newton's death, and there are suggestions that similar arrangements were in place in Spain before then, there is no hard-and-fast evidence of 'prior art' by the ancient Egyptians or anyone else. Sadly, therefore, this remains an unproven claim, since we can't be sure whether Newton did ever use a cat flap, and if he did, whether he was the first to do so.

The most compelling argument for the story's veracity is that Isaac Newton went to school in Grantham: an upbringing in a town of such uninterrupted boredom may have forced him to seek any alternative means of entertainment he could come up with, such as cutting holes in doors.

## VERDICT: FRUSTRATING

An equally random claim about Isaac Newton is that as a teenager he invented a mill powered by mice, perhaps the inspiration for the toy mill presented by the Mice on the Mouse Organ in the 1974 children's TV series *Bagpuss*. The mice claimed to be able to manufacture chocolate biscuits using only 'butter beans and breadcrumbs' – Isaac Newton would no doubt have refuted their claims slightly more quickly than did stuffy woodpecker-shaped book-end Professor Yaffle.

## Fanta was invented in Nazi Germany

YOU MIGHT NOT KNOW THAT FANTA, a brand owned by The Coca-Cola Company, is available in a bewildering number of flavours: something like 70 worldwide, including such delicacies as corn, vanilla cream, cinnamon rum, tamarind, bubble gum and bitter water. (*Bitter water?* 'Hey kids, try some of this soft drink: it tastes like water but a bit unpleasant.')

Equally, you might not know that if it hadn't been for Adolf Hitler, you wouldn't be able to enjoy the drink that evokes 'happiness and special times with friends and family', according to its makers. Let's be clear about this, though, and lawyers take note: Fanta was not invented 'by a Nazi'; it was not invented 'by the Third Reich'; and it was not invented 'for the Nazis'. It happened to be invented in Nazi Germany during the Second World War, by Coca-Cola GmbH, the German branch of the Coke empire. Then again, Coca-Cola's conduct before and during the war was not entirely uncontroversial.

In contrast to the post-war image of Coca-Cola as a brand representing the American way of life everywhere in the world, during the 1930s Coca-Cola was carefully marketed in Germany so as not to emphasise its American heritage. (A popular – and possibly bogus – story that emerged after 1945 told how German prisoners of war arriving in New Jersey were amazed to discover that Coke was available in the US, having believed it was a German drink.) Coke's sales grew from strength to strength in the lead-up to war, with their target market being industrial workers, who were having to put in more hours and therefore needed more refreshment than ever. By 1939, ten years after its launch in that country, over four million cases of Coke were sold annually in Germany.

While Coca-Cola GmbH could hardly be accused of actively supporting the ideals of the National Socialists, they were certainly more than happy to collaborate with the Nazi regime in selling as much Coke as they could and associating themselves with the swastika when it might help to boost sales – including prominent support for the 1936 Olympic Games in Berlin. During the war, the head of Coca-Cola GmbH, Max Keith, was appointed to the Office of Enemy Property, thereby able to control the takeover of Coca-Cola plants in the countries that came to be occupied by Hitler. When the US joined the war, however, the American president of The Coca-Cola Company, Robert Woodruff, famously pronounced: 'We will see that every man in uniform gets a bottle of Coca-Cola for five cents, wherever he is and whatever it costs our company.' This was heralded as both a marketing coup and a patriotic gesture – although technically he didn't specify every man in an *American* uniform.

Was the behaviour of Coca-Cola all that sinister? Before the war, with the intent of the Nazi Party not necessarily obvious to onlookers, it's reasonable to assume that Coca-Cola was as eager as any other company in any other country to sell their products to the government and to anyone else who wanted to part with their cash. And you could argue that any company wanting to continue to survive – and avoid nationalisation – in wartime Germany could not possibly avoid dealing with the authorities. On the other hand, you could also argue that the Americans owning the majority of Coca-Cola GmbH had the choice of withdrawing from the market when the US joined the war in 1941. In fact, that's pretty much what happened, albeit through the impracticality of maintaining normal dealings between the American owners and the German subsidiary.

Early on in the war, it became clear to Max Keith that American supplies of the various ingredients for Coca-Cola would soon be cut off, as would any contact with his bosses, so he got busy inventing a new fruit-flavoured soft drink that counted caffeine, cheese whey and cider residue among its ingredients. A contest to name the new drink ended within seconds of Keith inviting his employees to use their imagination – *Phantasie* in German. Rather than doing so, someone just suggested the abbreviated word 'Fanta' as the name, probably so they could knock off early for the day.

In 1945, with defeat looming, the Ministry of Commerce told Max Keith that Coca-Cola GmbH would finally be nationalised and that if he refused he would be sent to a concentration camp. Keith duly refused, but never had to test his resolve because the general in charge of the Ministry was killed by an air raid before the deadline was up. Once the war had ended, American representatives of The Coca-Cola Company were delighted to find out about the new Fanta brand, which had proved to be highly popular from the outset.

## VERDICT: TRUE

The Coca-Cola Company finally decided to introduce Fanta to the US in 1960.

# Margaret Thatcher made
# Mr Whippy ice cream possible

SHORTLY AFTER BECOMING Secretary of State for Education
and Science under Edward Heath's government in 1970, Margaret
Thatcher caused controversy by ending the provision of free milk
to schoolchildren, a decision that tabloid newspapers kept going on
about for decades afterwards. So it would be an irony as delicious as
a Flake 99 to discover that Britain's future prime minister had
invented a dairy-based product so popular with children. Then
again, when you grow up in the moribund Lincolnshire town of
Grantham, as the then-Margaret Roberts did, perhaps experimenting with ice cream is the exciting alternative to facing the
reality of a place whose claim to fame is that it used to be a major
railway junction. In other words, perhaps Mr Whippy was
Thatcher's equivalent to the cat flap (see p. 172).

In fact the Iron Lady had left Grantham by the time she started
dabbling in ice cream. There are a few variations on the claim, for
example that Maggie Thatcher developed Mister Softee ice cream,
or that she simply *invented ice cream* (blatantly false). The truth is
that after studying chemistry at Oxford University she worked for
the now-defunct plastics firm British Xylonite, before landing a
job in research and development for the food giant Lyons, at a time
when Lyons was an exceptionally successful and innovative
business. Best known for tea shops, corner houses, cakes and ice
cream, Lyons also ran hotels and restaurants, operated a war-time
munitions factory in Bedfordshire on behalf of the government,
and were famous for developing LEO (the Lyons Electric Office).

LEO was the world's first business computer, developed with assistance from Cambridge University. It's perhaps difficult today to believe that the British tea shop empire beat IBM in the race to automate what nowadays would be called 'supply-chain management' and 'payroll outsourcing'.

One of her team's accomplishments at the Lyons laboratory was to develop new ways to rip off consumers by adding more air to the product, hence requiring less actual ice cream in the manufacturing process. This resulted in what is known as 'soft-serve' ice cream, with a lighter texture that actually proved very popular and which enabled companies like Messrs Whippy and Softee to dispense ice cream from machines, rather than having to scoop it out of a vat. The research chemist documented her findings on the subject of 'fat extension' in a paper on the elasticity of ice cream.

Not long afterwards, around 1951, Thatcher made a significant career decision, ditching dairy products and food additives, and instead studying to become a barrister. After being called to the bar (insert your own joke about her husband Denis here), by the end of the decade she had chosen another occupation again, being elected as the MP for Finchley in 1959. Her prominence on the British political scene steadily grew until she reached the top of the tree by becoming the country's first female prime minister 20 years later. By 1990, with her public support melting away, she was frozen out by her own party and finally resigned.

The progress of Lyons was rather less spectacular. Their computing division was sold in 1963 to English Electric, which was later absorbed into ICL – now part of Fujitsu. The food and catering business was in sharp decline by the 1970s, being bought out by Allied Breweries, and the Lyons Maid ice cream brand was eventually gobbled up by Nestlé in the early 1990s.

## VERDICT: TRUE
Francis Rossi nearly went into the family ice cream business before achieving chart success with Status Quo.

# In seventeenth-century Holland, a tulip could cost you as much as a house

A COMMON 'TOURIST'S-EYE VIEW' of the Netherlands today – setting aside for a moment hard drugs and sex museums – is the colourful prospect of fields full of tulips. Thousands of them. It seems difficult to believe that some 400 years ago, these could have represented a cash crop that might have made the country the richest on the planet.

It's the fact that certain varieties of tulip *weren't* available by the field-load that made them – for a while – exceptionally valuable in the Dutch provinces during the 1630s. In fact, at the time, the United Provinces (later to emerge as the modern-day Netherlands) represented the world's dominant trading nation, certainly a contender for being the richest. The wealth generated from international commerce, which centred on the up-and-coming city of Amsterdam, in combination with a relatively high tolerance for intellectual and religious differences, led to a spectacular flourishing of science and the arts as the seventeenth century progressed. It was the so-called Golden Age of Rembrandt, Huygens and Descartes (who lived and worked in Holland from 1628 to 1649).

It wasn't quite so 'golden', however, if you were on the wrong end of one of the main economic drivers of the time, the slave trade.

All this cash meant people were looking for 'investment opportunities', and what better concept than the tulip? The flower is believed to have been introduced to the Low Countries in the 1590s by botanist and doctor Carolus Clusius (also known as Charles de l'Ecluse), who had got hold of some bulbs from the Ottoman Empire. Elaborate breeding, especially with the controlled introduction of a virus that caused flame-like patterns on the flowers' petals, led to numerous rare and extravagant varieties emerging, which were highly prized by the wealthy upper classes. As traders jumped on the bandwagon, exploiting the fact that people were prepared to pay vast amounts of money for this must-have accessory, 'tulipmania', or 'tulipomania', emerged.

Soon tulips were traded even before they had become flowers: while the bulbs were still growing in the ground or often before planting, they were bought and sold for small fortunes via promissory notes, creating what famously became known as *windhandel* ('trading in the wind'), because of the invisible nature of the commodity. If this seems confusing, think of these deals as the forerunners of modern-day futures contracts. If that seems even more confusing, just watch the scene in *Trading Places* when the Dukes explain about coffee, wheat, pork bellies, frozen concentrated orange juice and gold, and Eddie Murphy mugs to camera.

At the height of tulipmania, deals were often made in terms of livestock and property rather than hard cash. The full effects of speculation can be seen by charting the progress of the most famous tulip variety, the elusive Semper Augustus. In his book *Tulipomania*, Mike Dash describes how the first known example, cultivated in northern France, was sold around 1614 for 'a pittance' to a mysterious Amsterdam collector, who by 1624 was turning down offers of up to 3,000 guilders a bulb. A small number of Semper Augustus bulbs, notoriously difficult to grow, did eventually become available in the marketplace again. By 1633 they were selling for 5,500 guilders a bulb, rising to the extraordinary price of 10,000 guilders a bulb in January 1637: enough money to buy, as Mike Dash puts it, 'one of the grandest homes on the most fashionable canal in Amsterdam', a city where property was perhaps the costliest in the world.

In February 1637, however, the tulip market crashed with astonishing speed and severity – and within a matter of days, many speculators found themselves facing bankruptcy and destitution. The full extent of tulipmania and the economic significance of the resulting crash are subjects of debate among historians today, but it's reasonable to compare the mounting tulip frenzy to the 'dot-com boom' of the late 1990s, when investors poured money into rubbish websites run by snowboarding-obsessed geeks, only to realise later that they had poured money into rubbish websites run by snowboarding-obsessed geeks.

## VERDICT: TRUE

The word 'tulip' comes from the Turkish pronunciation of the Persian word for 'turban'.

# Maupassant hated the Eiffel Tower so much that he left France

THE FRENCH WRITER Guy de Maupassant (full name Henri René Albert Guy de Maupassant, in case it comes up in next week's pub quiz) was 39 when the Eiffel Tower was officially opened on 6 May 1889, for the *Exposition Universelle* (World's Fair), and is believed to have roundly hated it for the remaining four years of his life. The literary theorist Roland Barthes opened his 1964 essay on the Paris landmark with the claim that Maupassant used to have lunch in the Eiffel Tower's restaurant on a frequent basis – because it was the only place in the city where he didn't have to look at the Eiffel Tower.

Did Maupassant really dislike it enough to run away? This pub fact was certainly propagated by the Russian writer Anton Chekhov in *The Seagull* (a play second only to Henrik Ibsen's *Hedda Gabler* in terms of its dancing-in-the-aisles feelgood ending). Chekhov, like Maupassant, earned a lasting reputation as a master of the short story genre, and in *The Seagull* his character Irina Nikolayevna Arkadina, the actress mother of the wannabe-writer Konstantin Gavrilovich Treplev, reads a passage from Maupassant's Côte d'Azur travelogue *Sur l'eau* (*On the Water*), which expresses some uncomfortable opinions about a situation similar to her domestic set-up. Prior to this, however, Treplev is moaning on about how modern theatre is clichéd and tedious, and says that sometimes it's so bad it makes him want to run away – just as Maupassant ran away from the Eiffel Tower because it was so vulgar. (Unfortunately for Chekhov, the audience's reaction to the 1896 premiere of *The Seagull* was pretty much how he'd described Maupassant's reaction to the Eiffel Tower – although like the latter, *The Seagull* became immensely popular in the century that followed.)

Maupassant's dislike for the structure had already become public knowledge when building work had barely started. In 1887, along with numerous other literary and artistic figures such as Charles Garnier, Leconte de Lisle, Alexandre Dumas *fils* and Charles Gounod, he signed a petition against the tower which was published in the newspaper *Le Temps*. Obviously this was to no avail, and Maupassant became even more infuriated as the tower neared completion. A year after its official opening, he published some travel notes in the form of *La Vie errante* (*The Wandering Life*), beginning with an explanation of why he decided to revisit the Italian city of Florence: 'I left Paris, and indeed France, because the Eiffel Tower annoyed me too much.' In an extended rant over several pages he described the landmark as a *squelette disgracieux* ('unsightly skeleton') and predicted, incorrectly as it turned out, that after seven months the Eiffel Tower would be getting fewer visitors than the Leaning Tower of Pisa was getting after seven centuries.

Maupassant didn't leave France for very long (and certainly not permanently, as some people claim), as by 1892, due to the suicidal effects of syphilis, he was confined to an asylum in Paris, where he died.

### VERDICT: TRUE

The half-sized replica Eiffel Tower built in front of the Paris Las Vegas hotel and casino, opened in 1999, was originally going to be an identical, full-sized copy, but had to be reduced due to concerns it was too near to McCarran International Airport.

## Ernie Wise made the UK's first mobile phone call

ERNIE WISE — real name Ernest Wiseman — will forever be remembered as one half of the legendary comic double-act Morecambe and Wise, the light-entertainment giants of British television from the 1960s until Morecambe's death in 1984. (Eric Morecambe's real name was John Eric Bartholomew; he took his stage name from the Lancashire town where he grew up.)

On New Year's Day 1985, Ernie Wise was to be found dressed in a bizarre eighteenth-century outfit, standing next to a stage-coach in St Katharine's Dock: one of the areas of London whose regeneration from run-down industrial dereliction to commercial property hot-spot epitomised the boom time – for some – of the 1980s. Another symbol of the era that would soon emerge was the mobile phone: by the end of the decade, if you weren't walking round bleating about share prices while holding a brick to your ear, you wouldn't be getting a personal audience with Gordon Gekko any time soon.

It was just this technology that the amiable Ernie Wise – who couldn't be further from the 1980s excesses of conspicuous consumption – was launching in St Katharine's Dock, making the country's first ever call with a mobile phone, to the headquarters of Vodafone in Newbury, Berkshire. (Clearly, some rather less famous engineer must have tested the system first, and there were doubtless numerous calls over parts of the network as it was readied for public use, but even the worst pub bore would not be churlish enough to discount Wise's 'firstness' on this count.) The first 'real' call by a member of the public was made the following day, and probably consisted of the sentence 'Sorry, I'm just about to go into a tunnel.'

The publicity stunt to raise awareness for this all-new technology meant the fledgling Vodafone would steal a march on their rival (BT's Cellnet, which was eventually to become O2) by nine days. Vodafone – the 'vo' for 'voice', the 'da' for 'data', and the 'f' rather than the 'ph' just to make it sound a bit tawdry – started out as part of the telecoms arm of Racal, the now-defunct defence firm, before becoming a separate business in 1991. By 2006

Vodafone was the world's biggest mobile telecommunications company, and also had the distinction of announcing the biggest loss in British corporate history: £21.92 billion including impairment charges (whatever they are).

Various forms of mobile phone technology, particularly in-car systems, had existed in the UK, US, Sweden, Finland and elsewhere for decades prior to the establishment of Britain's Cellnet and Vodafone networks. But Wise's crackly analogue call was the first made in the UK on a cellular network as we know it today, where handsets allow a fully continuous conversation, handing off across different network cell areas while on the move.

### VERDICT: TRUE

The Duke of Edinburgh had Britain's only car phone in the 1950s, no doubt using it mainly to ask the Queen to put the kettle on when he was on his way home.

## Humpty Dumpty was a cannon

THE NURSERY RHYME about Humpty Dumpty is forever associated with an egg, even though the rhyme itself doesn't mention anything about eggs, or indeed make a whole lot of sense. Generally it is understood to be a riddle with the solution being an egg; although it is far from obvious why 'all the king's horses' should be involved in trying to put an egg back together. As Ricky Gervais commented in his *Politics* stand-up show, the only apparent moral of the verse is: 'Don't sit on a wall if you're an egg.'

The image of Humpty Dumpty that usually springs to mind is

John Tenniel's famous illustration for Lewis Carroll's *Through the Looking-Glass*. The opaque meaning of the nursery rhyme may be the reason why Lewis Carroll – real name Charles Lutwidge Dodgson – had his Humpty Dumpty character explain to Alice the meaning of the first verse of the equally baffling poem 'Jabberwocky', which she had read earlier in the story. On the other hand, if you believe the theories in Richard Wallace's extraordinary book *Jack the Ripper: Light-Hearted Friend*, Lewis Carroll was a mass murderer who was trying to draw attention to the fact that the opening stanza of 'Jabberwocky' is an anagram of an obscene foretelling of his crimes. (If you think that sounds ridiculous, rest assured that it's one of the least implausible theories in Wallace's book, which is definitely the most entertaining read in the Ripperology oeuvre.) But in *Through the Looking-Glass*, while Humpty Dumpty seems to 'morph' into existence from an egg, Alice gets into an argument with him: Humpty Dumpty says it is 'very provoking' to be called an egg, whereas she contends that she only said he *looked* like an egg.

Alice's comment acknowledges the fact that 'humpty dumpty' was, from at least the 1780s onwards, an informal term for – as the *Oxford English Dictionary* so eloquently puts it – 'a short, dumpy, hump-shouldered person'. It was also, however, the name of a vile-sounding drink of 'ale boiled with brandy' – and so it's interesting that the first depiction of Humpty Dumpty as an egg character, an 1843 illustration by an unknown artist, shows Humpty Dumpty falling off the wall as a result of drinking booze.

Like most nursery rhymes, the real origins of the Humpty Dumpty verse are lost in folklore, but it has often been argued that the rhyme started life as a riddle about a particular public figure.

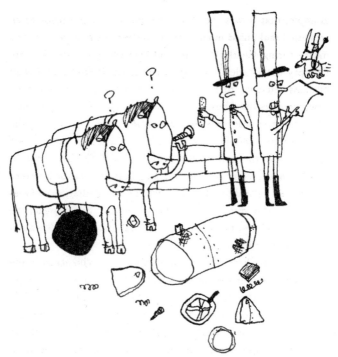

For example, Richard III, who was said to be hunch-backed (although historians question whether this was actually the case) fell from his horse and was killed at the Battle of Bosworth Field, which would explain the 'all the king's horses and all the king's men' line. However, the earliest printed version of the rhyme, in *Gammer Gurton's Garland* of 1810, does not mention a king at all: the third line is 'Threescore men and threescore more'.

In addition to public figures, other suggestions have been that Humpty Dumpty was rather more mechanical in origin; for example, that it was the name of some sort of precursor to an armoured tank, used in an attempt to cross the river Severn, or a moat, during Charles I's reign. Others contend that Humpty Dumpty was Charles I himself, with the whole falling-off-a-wall business referring to his execution. A more persistent theory, however, dates the rhyme to 1648, shortly before Charles's demise. The story goes that a massive cannon, which had been given the name Humpty Dumpty in reference to its rotund appearance, was mounted on the tower of St Mary at the Walls church in Colchester (now an arts venue that plays host to Colchester's annual beer festival), under the command of a soldier called One-Eyed Jack Thompson. Due to enemy fire during the siege, the tower collapsed – and with it the cannon, which the Royalists tried to reassemble in vain.

As with the Richard III theory, there's no evidence that the original version of the rhyme made reference to 'all the king's horses and all the king's men', and equally it's entirely possible that the cannon could have been named in tribute to the nursery rhyme. The cannon story is unlikely to be the genesis of the Humpty Dumpty verse, but there is, unfortunately, no way to know the definitive origin of the rhyme until historians unearth an ancient manuscript titled *Confessiones of a Nurserie Rime Author; or: A Most Excellente Treatise on the Subject of How I Did Wryte Humptie Dumptie and the Meaninge I Did Thereby Intende.*

## VERDICT: UNPROVEN

Manufactured by Gottlieb in 1947, the first pinball machine to feature an electrically powered flipper – or in fact, six of them – was called Humpty Dumpty; in a scene that would make Lewis

Carroll proud, during gameplay the king's bikini-clad 'ladies in waiting' on the backglass used brightly coloured streamers to pull an animated Humpty Dumpty off a wall.

## Francis Bacon died after stuffing a chicken with snow

WE'RE TALKING ABOUT the Elizabethan philosopher, statesman and essayist here, not the twentieth-century painter, although the modern Francis Bacon did claim to be a distant relative of his namesake.

Bacon was noted for his scientific focus on empiricism – understanding how the world works through experimentation and first-hand observation – and ultimately this is what cost him his life, when trying out a new form of food preservation. He was many years ahead of his time. The freezing of food did not become a widespread process until the invention of a quick-freezing technique in the early twentieth century by Clarence 'Bugs' Birdseye, who really was called Birdseye and wasn't just some creepy, big-bearded invention of the company now known as Birds Eye Foods. (He was a bit creepy, though: he is known to have eaten starlings, beaver tail and lion, and once recommended the 'excellent' taste of 'the front half of a skunk'.)

The first biography of Francis Bacon was published in Paris by Pierre Amboise in 1631, and simply states that he died as a result of staying outdoors too long during a severe frost, observing some unspecified phenomena. For the chicken story we have to turn to the description of Bacon's death provided by John Aubrey. The biographical sketches published today as Aubrey's *Brief Lives* were fragmentary notes prepared mainly for later use by his one-time friend Anthony Wood and were not intended to be published in their surviving form. They contain numerous notes reminding himself to check details, and are packed full of what can only be described as gossip: if published at the time, Aubrey's work would have constituted the seventeenth-century equivalent of the *National Enquirer* or *Heat* magazine. For example, he unhesitatingly states that Francis Bacon was homosexual; whether true or not, it would have been unimaginable to get away with publishing such an allegation during Aubrey's lifetime and not end up in prison (or worse).

Despite their informal and half-finished style, the *Brief Lives* give us a fascinating insight into the celebrities of Aubrey's time, due to the fact that he was extremely well connected. He was a close acquaintance of the philosopher Thomas Hobbes, who told him the detail of Bacon's demise. Driving through snow in a coach on the way up to Highgate, then a separate village to the north of London, Bacon wondered whether snow might preserve meat in the way that salt had been used. He bought a hen, had it gutted, and then stuffed it full of snow. He developed a severe cold and had to be taken to the Earl of Arundel's Highgate house, where he died a few days later; Aubrey gives the final cause of death as 'suffocation', which could indicate pneumonia. While a letter written by Bacon to the Earl of Arundel once he had reached the house (explaining why he was there) doesn't mention chicken-stuffing specifically, it does mention experimentation involving the 'conservation and induration of bodies'.

A somewhat safer food-related experiment would have been to

invent the Bacon Sandwich, although he couldn't have called it that, since he died over a hundred years before the meat-inside-two-bits-of-bread concept would come to be named after John Montagu, the fourth Earl of Sandwich.

## VERDICT: TRUE

In 1998 the musician Gerald Barry composed a work called 'Snow is White', inspired by the chicken-related circumstances of Francis Bacon's death.

# SPORTS

## Some golf balls contain honey

THE LEARNED BODIES WHO ARE responsible for the official rules of golf – the United States Golf Association in the US and Mexico, and the Royal and Ancient Golf Club of St Andrews everywhere else – lay down some strict guidelines about the size and shape of the ball. (Technically, since 2004 the Royal and Ancient Golf Club of St Andrews is now purely a private golf club, with the management of the golfing rules and the running of The Open Championship undertaken by a shadowy organisation known as The R&A. Okay, so it's not actually shadowy at all.)

A golf ball must weigh no more than 45.93 g (1.62 ounces), although there is no minimum weight. Conversely, there is no maximum diameter, only a minimum diameter of 42.67 mm (1.68 inches), and there are some odd instructions about how to prove, if necessary, that your ball meets the minimum requirement: it must drop through a ring gauge with a diameter of 1.68 inches 'in fewer than 25 out of 100 randomly selected positions' at a temperature of 23°C (plus or minus one degree). So, theoretically, if there was some sort of gentleman's disagreement about the size of your equipment, you might have to pick it up and drop it 100 times to demonstrate your point.

The ball must also be spherical, or at least have the properties of a 'spherically symmetrical ball', which means it is fine to manufacture a dimpled ball as long as it's symmetrical. Apparently dimpled golf balls fly further than non-dimpled golf balls; and there are some guidelines about the maximum overall distance a ball can travel, in order to maintain a certain level of skill in the game. If the ball becomes cracked or out of shape at any point, it is deemed to be unfit for play, and finally you can't apply 'foreign material' to a ball in order to change its playing characteristics.

With this level of regulation about the ball, it's no wonder The R&A's official rules run to over 190 pages (although the extent is not helped by the inclusion of six pages of adverts for Rolex). Nevertheless, there are no guidelines about what the ball can be made of or what colour it should be, so technically you could delicately balance a giant soap bubble on the tee and still be within the rules (until you swiftly fall foul of the whole 'unfit to play' business when you take a stroke, or when your opponent challenges you to the diameter test).

There would be nothing to stop you creating a ball with honey in the middle, and in the twentieth century enterprising golfers did start creating balls with liquid centres. Specifically, in 1906 a bank teller called Frank Hedley Mingay, from Renfrewshire in Scotland, was granted a UK patent ('An Improvement in Balls for use in the Game of Golf') which enabled him to create a golf ball whose core was a spherical bag containing 'an incompressible fluid such as water, glycerine, treacle, &c.' He obviously had to fine-

tune it by adding
powder into the mix, because
the following year he was granted
another patent ('An Improved
Golf Ball') for the creation of golf
balls whose core would contain a
mixture of a liquid and a pulverised
material, where such liquid might
involve water or 'glycerine, treacle,
dextrin, beer, or stout'. So by extension, yes, honey could have
been used – but surely the headline-grabber here is that you could
create a golf ball with a Guinness core?

The only significant usage of honey in golf balls was in the Hagen
range brought out in the 1930s by the L.A. Young Golf Company
of Detroit, who used the slogan 'Bees Buzz into Big Business' on
one of their brochures. The honey concept didn't stick, however.

All this was decades ago, and while patents for the creation of liquid-centre golf balls have been granted as recently as 1992 (to Bridgestone Corporation, for example), when liquids are used in modern-day golf balls they tend to contain water, glycerine (which means golf balls are made from peanuts – see p. 97) or related substances such as an aqueous ethylene glycol solution, which is a type of antifreeze. In recent years the trend has been very much away from liquid cores. A typical ball nowadays might have some kind of high-tech solid core, such as a titanium compound, or a more traditional soft-wound rubber core, or it might have a water-filled core wrapped in rubber yarn – perhaps even containing some corn syrup – but it *won't* contain honey.

## VERDICT: FALSE

In the early seventeenth century, the 'featherie' ball replaced the early wooden type of golf ball, and consisted of a leather bag stuffed with exactly one top-hat-full of boiled goose feathers.

# Marvin Hagler's real name is Marvelous Marvin Hagler

THE FORMER BOXER, who was world middleweight champion from 1980 to 1987, was born Marvin Nathaniel Hagler in Newark, New Jersey, and grew up in Brockton, Massachusetts – the birthplace of Rocky Marciano (whose real name was Rocco Marchegiano). Like many boxers, Hagler adopted a nickname ('The Marvelous One') to make the sport sound more interesting than it really is; but on 23 April 1982 he took things a step further by legally changing his name to Marvelous Marvin Hagler at Plymouth Probate Court, Massachusetts. So technically, while Marvelous Marvin Hagler is (obviously) not his birth name, it is indeed his real name.

The reasoning given at the time was that Hagler was irritated when ABC billed him as simply 'Marvin Hagler' – only referring once in passing to the fact that locals called him 'Marvelous' – during his televised title defence against Caveman Lee in Atlantic City in March of that year. (ABC chose the opposite policy when referring to his opponent as simply 'Caveman Lee', although in the introduction, commentator Keith Jackson did tell viewers that his real name was William and that he owed his nickname to the amount of hair he sported when he was younger.) According to the *New York Times*, when Hagler's attorney challenged a representative of the TV company, the response was: 'If he wants to be called Marvelous Marvin at ABC, tell him to go to court and have his name changed.' And that's exactly what he did.

Caveman Lee also went to court the following year, but for very different reasons, after robbing a bank – an activity for which he has served three jail sentences.

## VERDICT: TRUE

Musa Ngozo, a boxer from Swaziland who competed at the 2006 Commonwealth Games in Melbourne, legally changed his name to Musa Swissroll Ngozo in tribute to his favourite food.

# They measure Super Bowl viewing figures by flushing the toilet

EVERY YEAR, SUPER SUNDAY GIVES Americans an excuse to watch TV in record numbers while indulging in beer-guzzling and snack-munching on an epic scale; all in the name of watching grown men run around in shoulder pads and in the additional hope of glimpsing a 'wardrobe malfunction' during the half-time show. Every year, someone will tell you that the Super Bowl attracts 'a billion viewers worldwide'. The more adventurous sports enthusiast/amateur network executive will claim that the most accurate way to measure the actual audience figures is not by monitoring TV sets or otherwise recording viewing habits, but by water companies *measuring the number of toilets that are flushed during the breaks*.

Of course, viewing figures aren't just a shoddy means to try to convince the rest of the world that anyone bothers watching such a dull sport. It's really about Big Bucks: the higher the audience figures, the higher the advertising fees. For Super Bowl XLI in 2007 the going rate for a 30-second commercial spot during the game was reportedly $2.6 million. If you've spent that much on a crappy advert, the last thing you want is to be flushing your market share down the pan.

There certainly is a surge in toilet-flushing during commercial breaks in popular programmes, but even Heath Robinson couldn't construct a system elaborate enough to accurately measure how many flushes there were across all the households of America and link that to what had been on TV. Nevertheless, a related rumour

persists that each year, especially at half-time, America's sewerage systems reach breaking point due to the amount of, er, 'waste' being disposed of. For the 2006 Super Bowl, Scott Tissue – who just happen to make toilet paper – created a website, halftimeflush.com, to cash in on the idea that many households suffer blockages during the Big Game. And there *was* a water main failure in Salt Lake City during the 1984 Super Bowl, but the outage was never confirmed as being caused by the breaks in the game and was probably co-incidental.

The way that 'they' actually measure viewing figures for TV pro-grammes and commercials is a little more sanitary, but arguably not much more accurate. Data is gathered via Nielsen Media Research and similar organisations using meters connected to TV sets and other home-entertainment devices, allowing them to see what kinds of people (and not just how many) are watching which shows. Well, so we're told, anyway: have you ever been round to someone's house and seen any such device plugged into the TV?

So, regardless of their toilet habits, how many people do tune in for the Big Game? According to Nielsen, the total 2007 Super Bowl figure was 93.2 million – second only to the 1996 Super Bowl and 1983's final episode of *M\*A\*S\*H* in terms of record viewer numbers.

Incidentally, if you're the company who has stumped up for some air time to advertise your product – plus the cost of making the commercial and any associated marketing – you're interested in far more than just the number of people who would have been watching your spot: website hits, press clippings, blog entries and data collected by market research firms to gauge prominence among 'water-cooler talk' are all things you'd be looking at, while everyone else is busy on the toilet.

## VERDICT: FALSE

In 1971 *All in the Family* (the US adaptation of British sitcom *Till Death Us Do Part*) featured the first prime-time toilet flush on American television.

# Jacques Villeneuve won pole position in a Grand Prix race after practising on a video game

CANADIAN RACING DRIVER Jacques Villeneuve became Formula One world champion in 1997, his second season. Although he never won the championship again, he remained a significant (if disappointing) presence in the competition throughout the following decade, driving for Williams, BAR, Renault and Sauber, before retiring from Formula One in 2006.

Off the track, Villeneuve is known to be a big fan of computer games. In 1999 fellow driver Johnny Herbert described him as a 'games junkie' and an early enthusiast for interactive online gaming. But would a professional driver really use a video game to practise for a Grand Prix race? Apparently so: Villeneuve has described this method of preparation on a number of occasions. In 2005, for example, before racing the Bahrain circuit for the first time, he said he would 'play with an F1 video game that includes this track to get used to the layout'; the game in question must have been *Formula One 04* for the Sony PlayStation 2. He was particularly keen to get in the extra practice because he had not seen the race on TV in 2004, which was the first year a Grand Prix took place at the new Bahrain International Circuit (when Villeneuve had been 'between teams'). Villeneuve's decision to spend his time playing computer games – rather than trying to get hold of a video of the previous year's race – didn't pay off, ending up with eleventh position overall after having to retire shortly before the finish.

However, Villeneuve had much better luck during his first

season, when he practised on Microprose's *Grand Prix II* game (hailed by computer nerds for breaking new ground in the realism of its simulations) in preparation for the 1996 Belgian Grand Prix on the Spa-Francorchamps circuit. Although Villeneuve claimed to have qualified only around eighteenth in the video game, he credited this virtual run with his success in achieving pole position in the real qualifying session. He didn't do too badly in the race itself, either, finishing in second place behind Michael Schumacher. On the occasions during Villeneuve's career when he crashed, he must have been astonished to discover that he didn't just reappear in the middle of the track as a flashing car.

The official Formula One games let you select which driver you want to race as, and perhaps Villeneuve may have tried to get inside his opponents' heads by choosing them when gaming. Ironically, in many of the games he couldn't have chosen to drive as *himself*, since for several years his management withheld permission for the licensing of his name or likeness in the official games.

## VERDICT: TRUE

Jacques Villeneuve owns a restaurant and club in Montreal called Newtown – an English rendering of his French surname (and his nickname in motor racing circles) which caused controversy among some French-speaking citizens of Quebec, who actually bothered complaining to the authorities to try to prevent the establishment having an English name.

## The ancient Egyptians invented bowling

THERE IS A SLIGHTLY BAFFLING RANGE of different varieties of bowling, such as duckpin, candlepin and five-pin, all of which involve rolling a ball at some pins and knocking them over. These types of 'bowling' are not to be confused with lawn bowls (and similar games such as bocce and pétanque, a form of boules), in which you try to get your ball as near as possible to another, smaller ball, usually known as the 'jack'.

The most popular form of bowling nowadays is of course tenpin, which evolved in America from various types of nine-pin skittles games imported from Europe. The increase from nine to

ten pins was perhaps just part of the American obsession of making everything bigger than anywhere else, as with cars, meals and mushrooms (see p. 41). If you live in Ireland and bring out an eleven-pin version of bowling, some enterprising sports nut in America will probably get wind of it and bring out a twelve-pin version called 'supermassively extreme megastructure maximum overdrive bowling'.

The European skittles games originated in Germany, where *Kegelsport* began in religious institutions around the fourth century AD, and quickly gained favour among the wider public. For a long time the number of pins was the same as the number of players in the game, until the somewhat unlikely bowling enthusiast Martin Luther spent time determining that nine was the ideal number (when not busy setting up a worldwide Protestantism movement).

Prior to the German *Kegel* craze, the Romans enjoyed something similar to bocce, and the ancient Polynesians played a bowling game called *ula maika*. But the oldest bowling paraphernalia found so far – dated to around 3200 BC – was discovered in an Egyptian tomb at Naqada by the archaeologist Sir William Matthew Flinders Petrie (who, as his middle names indicate, was the grandson of the Matthew Flinders who was the first person to circumnavigate Australia, at the start of the nineteenth century). Petrie's conclusion was that the find, which included four diorite balls, nine conical 'skittles' of breccia and limestone and three blocks of marble which could create a small archway, consisted of a bowling game. While there's no reason to doubt that – and see for yourself if you have a chance to visit Oxford's Ashmolean Museum – there is not much evidence that bowling was a widespread pastime in ancient Egypt. In other words, although the Egyptians got there first, it was the mediaeval German *Kegler* whom we really have to thank for the spread of vast provincial bowling alleys that stink of sweat and onion rings.

**VERDICT: TRUE**
The ancient Egyptians are not believed to have invented red and blue smelly shoes.

## Honduras and El Salvador went to war because of a World Cup result

AH FOOTBALL, 'the beautiful game'. That must have been what was going through Andrew Lloyd Webber's mind (along with dollar signs) when he decided to write a musical with Ben Elton called *The Beautiful Game*, in which football, or soccer, is used to 'tackle' the big political issues of Northern Ireland. (The show, which premiered on the London stage in 2000, apparently came about because Elton bluntly confronted the king of musical adaptations in 1998 with the question: 'Would you ever consider writing a musical with an original story?') Set in 1969 as 'The Troubles' were beginning, and featuring knee-capping and sectarian murder, it seems a little over the top for football, doesn't it? Well, perhaps you'd think differently if you were in Central America at the time when *The Beautiful Game* was set.

In 1969 the neighbouring countries of Honduras and El Salvador were both rather keen to qualify for the 1970 FIFA World Cup in Mexico. However, in reality the football was *not* the cause of what has come to be known as 'The Football War' or 'The 100

Aim....Fire..

Hours' War'. Rather, land reform laws enacted by Honduras led to the confiscation of land owned by the large number of Salvadoran immigrants, and rising tensions (fuelled in no small part by stories in the media of both countries about atrocities committed by the two regimes) led to El Salvador's army attacking Honduras on

14 July 1969, followed by four days of serious fighting on land and in the air. On 20 July, while Neil Armstrong was busy taking one small step on the moon, the Organization of American States negotiated a ceasefire – although a peace treaty wasn't finally signed until 1980, and the lasting effects of the war were around 4,000 fatalities, tens of thousands of displaced citizens and a prolonged suspension of the Central American Common Market. The two countries only finally signed an agreement on the border dispute arising from 'The Football War' in 1998, and in fact while normal diplomatic relations have resumed, the full implementation of the border demarcation agreement hasn't actually happened yet.

The football in June 1969 certainly added further tension to the already volatile atmosphere, in a build-up vividly described by the late Polish journalist Ryszard Kapuściński in his book *Wojna futbolowa* (translated by William Brand as *The Soccer War*). After the first World Cup qualifier in Tegucigalpa on 8 June 1969 (Honduras 1–0 El Salvador), an eighteen-year-old Salvadoran named Amelia Bolanios reportedly shot herself in the heart due to the shame of seeing 'her fatherland brought to its knees', with her televised funeral in San Salvador attended by the president and the Salvadoran national team. When the Hondurans came for the return match in San Salvador on 15 June (El Salvador 3–0 Honduras), they had to arrive at the stadium in armoured vehicles, with the game followed by rioting and beatings against the visiting fans, which reportedly resulted in at least two deaths. Finally, during a play-off on neutral ground in Mexico City on 26 June (El Salvador 3–2 Honduras), the two sets of fans at the stadium were separated by thousands of Mexican policemen, although the game itself remained relatively peaceful.

Now for the really important bit: you'd probably like to know what happened to El Salvador when they finally made it to the 1970 World Cup (after nearly being beaten to it by Haiti, who apparently used a witch-doctor to boost their chances). Well, after all that, the team never made it past the first round, having failed to score a single goal in their Group 1 fixtures against Belgium, the USSR and the Mexican hosts.

**VERDICT: FALSE**

The description of football as 'the beautiful game' owes its popularity to the 1977 publication of Pelé's autobiography *My Life and the Beautiful Game*, which was written with Robert Lloyd Fish (whose main line of business was writing mystery stories and, sometimes under the amusingly fish-based pseudonym Robert L. Pike, novels such as *Mute Witness*, which was later filmed as *Bullitt*).

## The first bicycle didn't have any pedals

WITH THE BENEFIT OF HINDSIGHT it's easy to scoff at some of the inventions that had a spark of potential – yet completely missed the point. In 1787, for example, Levi Hutchins, a 26-year-old clock-maker from Concord, New Hampshire, invented a mechanical alarm clock but failed to incorporate the means to set the time of the alarm: it always went off at 4 a.m., which was the time he liked to get up and go to work. (Presumably in his line of business the best strategy was to get in and out of work early, to avoid endless jibes from colleagues about being a 'clock-watcher'.) What's ridiculous about Levi Hutchins' invention is not just that he didn't realise its functional or commercial potential – but the fact that *the alarm clock had already been invented, with the ability to set the alarm*. Numerous mechanical alarm clocks of a more sensible nature had been constructed in Germany and England during the previous two centuries.

Enough about alarm clocks. A bicycle without pedals sounds pretty stupid, doesn't it? But that's exactly what the splendidly named Karl Friedrich Christian Ludwig Freiherr Drais von Sauerbronn invented around 1817. Incidentally, he wasn't always so splendidly named. In 1849, during the political changes in the German state of Baden, which were inspired by the revolution in Paris the year before, he changed his name to Bürger ('citizen') Karl Drais, as he was a committed democrat. Three months later he had to hastily change his name back again after the Prussians invaded. So maybe not *that* committed, you might be thinking – but it was a decision that had serious consequences: he was persecuted for his democratic beliefs and died two years later in poverty, after having his pension confiscated to help pay back the costs of the revolution in Baden.

Enough about revolutions, of the political kind, anyway. Drais' invention was the *Laufmaschine* – the running machine – and it looked like a bicycle, but the idea was that the rider would sit astride it and run with his feet. ('His' feet, because it was clearly not designed for use by anyone wearing a nineteenth-century dress.) The mainly wooden device, with its pivoting front wheel, enabled Drais to cover large distances quickly, and as the idea caught on, it became known variously as the velocipede, the draisine, the hobby-horse and (by the time it became the Regency Londoner's must-have accessory for summer 1819) the dandy-horse. A few years later, the vehicles were banned from many cities around the world as a public danger, and they fell out of fashion. Confusingly, the word draisine later came to refer only to curious pedal-powered vehicles that travel on railway tracks.

Although there are various other rumours as to possible antecedents of the modern-day bicycle, the *Laufmaschine* is the only clear-cut example of such an invention (it even featured a rudimentary brake) and it went on to inspire the penny farthing and the pedal-powered designs we're rather more familiar with today.

## VERDICT: TRUE

One unsubstantiated theory as to why Drais created the *Laufmaschine* when he did is that the eruption of Indonesia's Mount Tambora in 1815 led to the North European and North American climate problems and famines of the 'year without a summer' in 1816, sending the price of oats through the roof and making the search for a substitute horse a matter of urgency.

# GEOGRAPHY

## The letters 'c' and 'z' in European Spanish are pronounced differently to American Spanish because the king had a lisp

IF YOU DON'T SPEAK SPANISH, this whole claim may be rather baffling, so a little pub linguistics may be useful. In Spanish as spoken in Spain itself, the letter 'c' (when appearing before an 'e' or an 'i') and the letter 'z' are pronounced as the combination 'th' would be pronounced in the English word 'theophagy' – a word that the *Oxford English Dictionary* defines as 'the eating of god', whatever the hell that means. (Of course, in several dialects of English, this 'th' may be pronounced more like a hard 't', which is why linguists distinguish the sound in question as being a voiceless dental non-sibilant fricative.) In Spanish as spoken in the Americas, on the other hand, the written letters 'c' (when appearing before an 'e' or an 'i') and 'z' are pronounced as the letter 's' would be pronounced in the English word 'Spain'.

Numerous 'reasons' have been cited for this difference, usually involving some kind of ruler of Spain or the Iberian peninsula as a whole. The king had a lisp and everyone was in awe of him, so they all thought they'd better follow suit in order not to offend. Or they just thought it sounded cool so they imitated him and the fashion spread. Or he was a control freak and insisted that everyone around him spoke the same way he did. As to who the king in question was, well, maybe it was Philip II (who, confusingly, is known as Philip I in Portugal). Or it was Ferdinand (hey, there were so many King Ferdinands that this is a good way to avoid having to be too specific). Or it was just 'one of the Habsburg kings' in general.

The whole king story is total rubbish. Apart from the fact that there is no evidence for it whatsoever, we can be sure that the pronunciation is not the result of lisping because *otherwise the sound written as 's' would always be pronounced the same way*. In other words, the Spanish word *estupidez*, meaning 'stupidity', would always be pronounced as the English phonetic approximation 'eth-tupid-eth', rather than 'ess-tupid-eth'.

Nevertheless, it's not quite as simple as that. The above differentiation between European Spanish and American Spanish is actually far too clear-cut. In reality, there are dialects of Spanish spoken in Spain (in much of Andalusia, for example) where 'c' and 'z' are pronounced in the 'American' way, as 's'. And in other parts of Andalusia, particularly rural areas, *estupidez* would actually be pronounced as 'eth-tupid-eth' due to the phenomenon known as *ceceo*, whereby all the sounds written as 'c', 'z' and 's' are all pronounced like the English 'th'. Conversely, *seseo* is the name for the phenomenon in which 'c', 'z' and 's' are all pronounced like the English 's' ('ess-tupid-ess') which, as noted, is what happens in most of the dialects of Spanish spoken in the Americas – but not all of them. Confused? Just don't ask how speakers of these dialects actually pronounce the words *ceceo* and *seseo*.

## VERDICT: FALTH

Unrelated to the *ceceo* or the *seseo*, the title of the Phil Collins song 'Sussudio' was the name his daughter gave to her horse, although Collins has given conflicting explanations as to whether the horse was named after the song or vice versa.

# The guy who designed the Sydney Opera House has never seen it

BACK IN THE 1950S the New South Wales government ran a competition to design a new music venue, which was won in 1957 by a Danish architect called Jørn Utzon. Utzon's design for the building, while not yet fully developed, was recognised as ground-breaking and inspired, with its distinctive profile consisting of huge white sail-like shells. Two years later work got under way at the site on Bennelong Point, beside the harbour.

By the time construction of the podium was complete in 1962, the project was already experiencing significant delays. As work progressed and a new government took over in 1965, Utzon's relationship with New South Wales officials and various others became increasingly strained, and following a massive hissy-fit in 1966 he dramatically resigned from the project and left Australia a bitter man, swearing never to return.

Now, you might think that if you were in that situation, once, just once, you'd find some reason to go back to Australia a few

years later and sneak a peek. Surely you would be *just a little curious* to see how your dazzling design had worked out in reality. But no: true to his word, Jørn Utzon has never returned to Australia ...

This is probably a good thing, because what Utzon still doesn't know to this day is that after he left, no one could be bothered to realise his vision because the costs were spiralling out of control. So the New South Wales government knocked the half-finished opera house down and put in its place the Bennelong Point multi-storey car park, which is still there today. What you may not know is that the Australian authorities have spent the last few decades sending Jørn Utzon an elaborate series of faked photographs and tourist brochures about 'the Sydney Opera House' – even constructing whole web sites listing bogus opening hours and concert details, with Photoshopped images of how his design would have looked – so as to avoid getting sued by the bad-tempered architect.

Since 1966 this has required the funding of an Orwellian department solely dedicated to creating fake news and reports about 'the Sydney Opera House'. For years this was relatively straightforward – but the advent of the Internet, which made sharing information so much easier (particularly in terms of searching historical records), has meant that the department have had to massively ramp up their activities in the last decade. In February 2007 someone calculated that the total cost spent on this department has now exceeded even the most outlandish estimates of what the real building could have cost, and there is increasing pressure for government heads to roll.

At the turn of the millennium, following rumours that the gullible Utzon had been informed of the scam, the New South Wales government adopted a bold new strategy: to fend off Utzon's suspicions, they pretended to kiss and make up, allowing him to design a new 'Western Colonnade' – from his studio in Denmark – which they told him was opened by Queen Elizabeth

II in 2006. And they even pretended that they would remodel some of the interiors to reflect his original designs!

## VERDICT: TRUE

It's not just the Australian authorities who have been misleading Utzon; the international architecture community have also been complicit in the ongoing deception, and in 2003 they awarded him the prestigious Pritzker Prize.

# The Himalayas cover a tenth of the Earth's surface

THIS CLAIM – used by the BBC to promote their *Planet Earth* TV series in 2006 – is pretty bold when you consider that around 70 per cent of the Earth's surface is covered by water. If a further 10 per cent is taken up just with the Himalayas, that leaves only 20 per cent for 'lightweight' mountains like the Andes, the Alps and the Rockies, and flat or gently undulating stuff like prairies, plains, car parks, fens, foothills, ice rinks, steppes, low-level tundra, ten-pin bowling facilities and the Netherlands.

When you look at a map of the planet, it's clear that even if you take the broadest definition of the Himalayas (the entire mountain system that incorporates the Hindu Kush, the Pamir Mountains and the Karakoram range) there's no way that it could comprise a tenth of the Earth's surface, even if you're only talking about the bits above water. However, a map is two-dimensional, and most percentages quoted for surface area make the assumption that the Earth can be treated as if it were a smooth sphere, which is pretty much the case: as any man in the pub should know, if you were to reduce the Earth down to fit in the palm of your hand, then regardless of your Everests and your K2s, the planet would appear just as smooth as a billiard ball. However, even if you average out the extremities of the Earth's crust, it is not quite spherical, being slightly wider around the equator than from top to bottom, as if it had just eaten a large doner kebab, but without chips.

The 10 per cent claim becomes true when considering the surface of the Earth that is exposed to the atmosphere, as opposed to taking just a two-dimensional bird's-eye view. In other words, imagine if you took the Himalayas, along with the rest of the Earth's surface, and flattened everything out: the Himalayas become proportionally larger because of all those ups and downs.

The Himalayan mountain system is technically an orogenic belt, meaning that it's an example of mountains still being formed, as a result of the collision between the Indian tectonic plate and the Eurasian plate some 50–60 million years ago, give or take a year or two. This caused the land mass to crumple, eventually creating the Himalayas, which are still being pushed northwards, and which are also still rising at between 5 and 10 mm (0.2 and 0.4 inches) per year. So the proportion of the Earth's surface covered by the Himalayas is going up – literally – all the time.

## VERDICT: TRUE

In case you want to put it in your diary, 11 December has been designated International Mountain Day by the United Nations, as of 2003; apparently 2002's International Year of the Mountain was such a roaring success that they didn't want the party to stop.

## Pound for pound, hamburgers cost more than new cars

IN ORDER TO MAKE THIS CALCULATION vaguely sensible, let's choose the McDonald's Quarter Pounder for comparison, and let's assume you're buying it on its own and not as part of a 'meal deal'. In the UK in 2007 this would typically set you back £1.99 (roughly US$4.00 based on current exchange rates, although if you walk into a branch of McDonald's in the US, you'd probably be paying nearer $2.59 for it). This means you're paying around £7.96 per pound of burger. Okay, there will be a discrepancy between the cooked and uncooked weight of the patty, and there will be that weird bit of gherkin to contend with, but let's not overly complicate what is already a rather dubious mathematical computation.

The average cost of a new car in the UK in the same year was around £12,000, while the nation's most popular car was the Ford Focus, so that seems like a good reference point. There are always various promotions available, but the list price for a three-door Focus Studio started at £11,510 'on the road', though you could pay around £20,000 for a five-door Focus ST-3, whatever that might be. According to Ford, the lightest three-door Focus weighs 1,690 kg including a full tank of fuel and a driver weighing 75 kg. So take out the driver – assuming he or she doesn't come with the car – and you have a vehicle weighing 1,615 kg, or 3,560 pounds. Dividing £11,510 by 3,560 gives a cost-per-pound of £3.23. At the other end of the scale, if you've bought the most expensive five-door diesel model, having a without-the-driver weight of 1,875 kg (4,134 pounds), you're looking at £4.84 per pound of car.

So a pound of burger costs more than a pound of car. What exactly does this tell us? Anything?

## VERDICT: TRUE

Denny's Beer Barrel Pub in Clearfield, Pennsylvania, offers a range of extreme burgers, including a six-pound burger called The Ye Olde 96er™ at $35.95 (approximately £3.00 per pound); however, if you can eat it all within three hours they'll give you a T-shirt, a certificate and your money back – which would scupper the 'more expensive than a new car' claim.

## 'Taliban' just means 'students'

IF YOU HAD TO PINPOINT the start of the so-called War on Terror, it would be fair to say it kicked off in October 2001 when the US initiated 'Operation Enduring Freedom', hastily renamed from 'Operation Infinite Justice' on the basis that this might 'offend Muslims'. Even at the time, it seemed pretty clear that the *name* was hardly likely to be the operation's most controversial aspect.

The American administration's stated objectives of invading Afghanistan were to attack terrorist training camps and to depose the Taliban, whose leaders were believed to be sheltering Osama bin Laden. Just one month previously, before September 11 changed the world's focus, many people knew little about the Taliban, bin Laden or al-Qaeda, unless they remembered Bill Clinton's 1998 cruise missile attacks against suspected terrorist compounds in Afghanistan and the El Shifa Pharmaceutical Industries factory in Sudan, carried out in retaliation for the attacks on US embassies in Kenya and Tanzania.

After the Americans had undertaken the initial groundwork in Afghanistan, it fell to the International Security Assistance Force (ISAF) to take responsibility for stabilising – or at least attempting to stabilise – the situation from the start of 2002. Yet the War on Terror might suddenly seem a rather less frightening prospect if it turned out that the people ISAF found themselves fighting were actually just *a bunch of students*. For 'students' is indeed what the word 'Taliban' means: it's the plural form in Pashto (the language spoken in large parts of Afghanistan and

Western Pakistan) of the Arabic word for 'student', normally written as *talib* in the roman alphabet. So ISAF's best option to keep the Taliban at bay might be to set up a fake 'Fresher's Fair' event, luring the students with the promise of free beer and Pot Noodles, and then round them all up once they'd passed out from excessive alcohol consumption. Clearly some provision would need to be made to dispose of the large number of stolen traffic cones which the students would bring to the party.

Needless to say, the kind of students fighting in Afghanistan wouldn't be much interested in alcohol (although they are not known to have any specific ideological objection to Pot Noodles). The Taliban see themselves as students seeking knowledge of Islam, although their interpretations of Islam have been frequently debated; during their time in power the Taliban demonstrated their commitment to education by shutting down girls' schools.

## VERDICT: TRUE
In Arabic, 'al-Qaeda' means 'the base', and can communicate the sense of a foundation, a physical base of an object or shape, or a military base.

# There used to be an undersea post office in the Bahamas

THE BAHAMIAN POST OFFICE under the sea that was in operation between 1939 and 1942 owed its existence to the underwater film pioneer John Ernest Williamson, who was the cinematographer on the 1916 silent-movie version of Jules Verne's

*20,000 Leagues Under the Sea.* Initially taking inspiration from his father's invention of a tube to allow the flow of air and communication from a ship to a depth of some 75 metres (250 feet), Williamson devised highly successful ways to take underwater photographs before creating the Williamson Photosphere, which was a massive bulb-and-funnel contraption with a thick glass window designed to enable undersea filming. In 1914, together with his brother George, he captured the world's first underwater footage near Nassau in the Bahamas.

Some 25 years later Williamson was apparently still not bored of the whole underwater-movies concept and he led the scientific filming of the Bahamas–Williamson Undersea Expedition in 1939. At this stage the Photosphere was turned into 'the world's only undersea post office', and while it's not entirely clear what benefit there was to having the post office in the Photosphere itself, rather than just on the boat it was linked to, it fired the imagination of stamp collectors everywhere. The official postmark read 'Sea Floor, Bahamas', and if you're a philatelist who comes across a stamp marked in this way today, you'd probably get quite excited. Don't be confused, however, between stamps created in conjunction with the scientific expedition and a five-shilling commemorative stamp issued by the Bahamas in 1965, which features a picture of a man (presumably Williamson himself) merrily postmarking some letters while gazing out the window of the Photosphere.

## VERDICT: TRUE

There's a post office on board the International Space Station, allowing visiting cosmonauts and astronauts to use mission-specific postmarks; in 2003 the Russian Federal Space Agency announced they would charge private customers between US$20,000 and $30,000 per stamp.

# The Statue of Liberty is in New Jersey

LIBERTY ENLIGHTENING THE WORLD – to use the statue's official name – is situated on what is now known as Liberty Island, officially renamed from Bedloe's Island in 1956. A gift from the French to commemorate (belatedly) the centenary of the Declaration of Independence, the symbol of freedom and enlightenment was the brainchild of politician Edouard de Laboulaye and took physical form as the result of a collaboration between the sculptor Frédéric Auguste Bartholdi and the engineer Gustave Eiffel (whose tower Maupassant ran away from – see p. 184). It was constructed in France, shipped over to the USA in pieces, reassembled on site and declared open in 1886.

The island location, at the mouth of the Hudson River, was chosen as a welcoming point for New York City, and is permanently associated with New York. However, it is much closer to the neighbouring state of New Jersey than it is to Manhattan, and it clearly appears within the New Jersey state boundary as demarcated on maps, since the state boundary runs down the middle of the Hudson. Thus residents of New Jersey are keen to claim the statue as their own. Unfortunately for them, the official view of the National Park Service, who administer the site, is that Liberty Island is federal property 'located within the territorial jurisdiction of the state of New York'. The issue was clarified as part of an 1834 pact between the two states in which it was agreed that although the state boundary should run down the middle of the Hudson, the islands in New York harbour – including Staten Island and what is now Liberty Island – belonged to the state of New York.

New Jersey residents in a state of denial further point to the 1998 court case in which it was ruled that most of the nearby Ellis Island falls within New Jersey's boundaries. However, this was a ruling on the technicality of post-1834 landfill developments added to the existing island, and has no bearing on the status of Liberty Island. So the Statue of Liberty really is the symbol of New York that the rest of the world had always assumed it was.

## VERDICT: FALSE

At one stage, Liberty Island was known as Love Island, which could inspire an idea for a reality TV show: 12 celebrities could be 'ironically' locked up on Liberty Island and have to win their freedom by carrying out a number of degrading tasks.

# One per cent of Greenland's population lives in a single building

WITH A TOTAL POPULATION of around 57,000, Greenland, or Kalaallit Nunaat in the local Kalaallisut language, isn't exactly big. Or rather, it's not exactly big in terms of people, but in terms of area it's very big indeed, and is often claimed to be 'the world's biggest island' – although you could argue all day about whether the much bigger Australia counts as an island even though it's also a continent.

So 1 per cent of 57,000 is 570, which means this claim suddenly seems a lot more believable. But with all that space, you'd think the population could afford to spread out a little, even if over 80 per cent of the country is covered by ice. Unfortunately, though, the story of Greenland's population moving into drab apartment blocks is not one based primarily around choice. In the 1950s and 1960s the government of Denmark – whose sovereign is still Greenland's head of state, although since 1979 the island has been self-governed – decided it would be a great idea to try to modernise the economy. In principle perhaps not a bad intention, but in practice this involved closing down settlements and fishing villages and forcibly moving Inuit populations into large European-style blocks of flats, with new development centred on the capital city, Nuuk, known in Danish as Godthåb. (With a population of around 14,000, perhaps 'city' is too strong a word.)

Of the numerous apartment buildings constructed in Nuuk, Blok P – a long, six-storey oblong that could hardly be called 'inspiring' – was the biggest. First completed in 1966, with an extension built some five years later, the building now boasts over 20 apartments on each of five living floors. (Why build a five-storey block with apartments on the ground floor, when you could build a six-storey block with an apartment-free entrance level?) At one stage the building *was* home to over 515 people, making the '1 per cent' claim approximately correct. However, occupancy has declined over the years, to the extent that Blok P's total number of inhabitants was a mere 368 as of May 2007, which is bad news for pub statisticians: the proportion of Greenland's entire population who live there is now around 0.6 per cent.

Some of the social problems created by the changes in lifestyle associated with the move to the apartment blocks included increased levels of alcoholism, depression, suicide and violent crime. However, since the 1980s the authorities have been keen to tackle these issues through education and improved housing conditions, with a focus on smaller buildings and the use of brightly coloured paint, features that now dominate the overall visual style of Nuuk's architecture.

## VERDICT: FALSE

Nuuk boasts the world's largest post box, used for correspondence addressed to Santa Claus.

## Colgate means 'go hang yourself' in Spanish

BUSINESSES WHO MARKET THEIR PRODUCTS internationally often have to change brand names for different countries. Indeed it's standard practice to carry out market research on proposed brand names before launching them, to ensure that the name is deemed to be catchy and inoffensive in a particular language or region, and also to ensure that it won't be the same as, or confused with, an existing product. In some cases, as with the Nintendo Wii console, a company may deliberately choose a name that is risqué (in the mildest possible sense) as a talking point.

In Spanish, the verb *colgar* means 'to hang' and the use of a *-te* suffix on a verb whose infinitive ends in *-ar* creates the second person singular imperative form of the verb, meaning that it becomes a command to do something directed at the person the speaker is talking to (in other words, directed at 'you'). In European Spanish, however, the 'o' of the verb *colgar* modifies to become a 'u', and an 'é' gets added into the mix too. So to say 'hang yourself' or 'go hang yourself' in European Spanish you might say *cuélgate*.

For Spanish as spoken in Argentina, however, it's a different matter. No 'é' is added to the first vowel, and it doesn't become a 'u' either, which means that the corresponding verb form for 'go hang yourself' really is the simpler *colgate*, as in the toothpaste.

Nevertheless, European Spanish speakers have another word form, *colgarte*, which is very similar but in this case is not a command, but a single-word combination of the infinitive *colgar* with the personal pronoun suffix *te*, effectively meaning 'to hang you'. This then lends itself to a play on words, with the idea being that a laid-back speaker might drawl the toothpaste name Colgate as the word *colgarte*. So, armed with this knowledge of Spanish, here goes with the joke.

A bloke walks into a shop and lazily says to the assistant: *Quiero Colgate* ('I want Colgate', which, if drawled, could sound like *Quiero colgarte*, 'I want to hang you'). The assistant replies: *Y yo escupite, pegate y asesinate* (which sounds like *Y yo escupirte, pegarte y asesinarte*: 'And I want to spit on you, beat you up and murder you'). Genius.

The meaning of the word *colgate* hasn't, however, resulted in Colgate-Palmolive changing their name in Argentina.

## VERDICT: TRUE

A naming decision that really did force a branding change in Spain was the Mitsubishi Pajero, which was called the Mitsubishi Montero in Spanish-speaking countries because *pajero* means 'wanker'. (Confusingly, the Pajero was also marketed in the UK as the Mitsubishi Shogun and, under licence to Hyundai, as the Galloper in some territories.)

## The only country whose name begins with the letter 'a' but doesn't end with the letter 'a' is Afghanistan

NONSENSE, NONSENSE, NONSENSE, nonsense, nonsense. If anyone dares to run a pub quiz where 'Afghanistan' is the answer to a question about the only country in the world starting but not ending with 'a', wave this book in front of their face, demanding a 'steward's enquiry', and shout: *haven't you heard of Azerbaijan?* And don't accept any further nonsense about the 'official' name of Azerbaijan – the Republic of Azerbaijan – starting with an 'r', because the 'official' name of Afghanistan is the Islamic Republic of Afghanistan.

There are some other more contentious candidates, such as Åland and Ascension Island, but it's reasonable to argue that these are not really 'countries' in their own right. (The Åland islands, in the Baltic Sea, constitute an autonomous province of Finland, while Ascension Island is a dependency of Saint Helena – itself an overseas territory of the UK.)

## VERDICT: FALSE

Between 1922 and 1964 Ascension Island was run not by an Administrator, as present, but by the Eastern Telegraph Company, who then became Cable & Wireless – although between 1945 and 1981 Cable & Wireless was owned by the British government.

## The Pentagon has twice as many toilets as necessary

SIXTEEN MONTHS OF CONSTRUCTION BEGAN on the distinctive Pentagon building in Arlington, Virginia, on 11 September 1941 (conspiracy theorists take note), consolidating 17 previous buildings of what was then the Department of War and is now the Department of Defense. The 'largest low-rise office building in the world' is a working environment for some 23,000 military and civilian employees (plus 3,000 support staff not directly working for the Department of Defense), so the toilets – or restrooms, to stick with American terminology – were always going to be high on the agenda. They've certainly made the news over the years.

During the Reagan administration the Pentagon, under then-Secretary of Defense Caspar Weinberger, was responsible for a supposed spending waste in which it was claimed they were buying toilet seats at $640 a go. The justification at the time was that it was not actually a toilet seat but a 'plastic assembly covering the entire seat, tank and full toilet assembly' – although the Department of Defense did acknowledge that they had been overcharged by their supplier.

Prior to this, in 1972, a bomb destroyed a Pentagon toilet in an anti-Vietnam protest by the radical group known as the Weathermen (whose name, incidentally, was a tribute to the line 'you don't need a weatherman to know which way the wind blows' from Bob Dylan's 'Subterranean Homesick Blues').

But it's the *number* of toilets that is perhaps the most

controversial aspect of the Pentagon's lavatorial history. There are currently 284 restrooms in the complex. Exactly how many individual toilet stalls there are per restroom has not been confirmed, but history does tell us that twice as many as necessary were constructed – for a rather unamusing reason. As James Carroll explains in his 'biography' of the Pentagon, *House of War*, the man in charge of the building's construction, Leslie R. Groves, decided that the Pentagon should house racially segregated dining and lavatory areas, meaning that 'at each corridor junction, double toilet facilities would be built, separated by race'. In Groves' eyes, he was simply implementing the race policies set by the state of Virginia – but President Franklin D. Roosevelt had recently outlawed discrimination in the US armed forces, and after visiting the site and demanding to know why there were so many toilets, FDR ordered Groves to make them equal-opportunity restrooms. According to Carroll, this made the Pentagon the only place in Virginia where segregation was not allowed, for a period of some 14 years.

## VERDICT: TRUE

There are no windows on the top floor of the Pentagon, because they had already started building the roof on the floor below before they decided to stick an extra storey on top, by which point they didn't have time to factor in complicated stuff like windows.

# In England the Speaker of the House is not allowed to speak

THIS TOTALLY UNTRUE CLAIM is something you hear from time to time in the US, where they frequently cite it as an example of the quaint traditions of ye olde British institutions. Your average Brit, of course, loves to play up to the Americans' perceptions of quaintness by constantly pretending to be a polo buddy of Prince William and putting on an upper-crust accent when phoning to book a restaurant table.

The US House of Representatives has its own Speaker of the House, which is why the supposed no-speaking rule in the British House of Commons seems to be such an amusing contrast. Historically, the American Speaker of the House position was a borrowing from the British political system. Just like the American counterpart, and the similar posts in the Canadian House of Commons, the New Zealand House of Representatives, the South African National Assembly and the Australian House of Representatives, the role of the British Speaker of the House is to moderate debate and enforce the rules of the assembly. Duties include choosing who can speak next, deciding whether to allow emergency debates and ruling on complaints. Normally the Speaker must remain impartial and therefore is not allowed to vote, which is probably where the confusion about not speaking crept in, particularly since the American equivalent is very much a party-political role. However, in the British system if there's a tie, the Speaker has to cast the deciding vote.

In fact, much of the time the Speaker's job as Chair is carried out

by deputies, since typical hours when the Speaker works in the
House of Commons chamber are the first two hours of the day from
Monday to Thursday, one hour in the evenings and other occasional times throughout the week. You might think the Speaker is
whiling away the rest of the time in one of the numerous bars in the

Palace of Westminster, but in fact the Speaker acts as the representative of the House of Commons in dealings with the House of Lords and external bodies – and to maintain impartiality the Speaker 'does not frequent the Commons dining rooms or bars', according to the House of Commons Information Office. Not only that, but the Speaker has other more 'normal' tasks associated with being an MP, like responding to constituents' letters and evading difficult questions, although traditionally the Speaker resigns from his or her party on taking up the post, to minimise political bias.

Most famously, when debates get a little hot-headed, the Speaker has to shout 'Order! Order!' to maintain a sense of decorum in the House – otherwise all the childishly bickering MPs would probably end up pulling each other's hair and squirting ink cartridges around.

## VERDICT: FALSE

The House of Commons Information Office is also keen to tell us that upon taking office in October 2000 the 156th Speaker, the Right Honourable Michael Martin, chose not to wear the Speaker's traditional knee breeches or silk stockings but a black flannel trouser instead.

## Ravioli means 'little turnips' in Italian

LIKE 'PANINI' AND 'GRAFFITI', 'ravioli' is one of those Italian words that, having been transported into English, have to be used in their plural forms unless you want to sound like a pompous idiot. Should you wish to be greeted by a blank stare or a wry smirk, go into a British sandwich shop and ask for 'a panino'. If you describe a particularly striking piece of street art as 'an urban graffito' then you probably work for *Time Out* magazine. And your parents never told you to make sure you ate every raviolo on your plate. You can, however, just about get away with a legitimate use of the singular if you're a chef who has created a dish consisting of one large raviolo, because if you put 'ravioli' on the menu you might get complaints from customers expecting something more.

So if you asked for *ravioli* in an Italian restaurant, would you end up with a plate of little turnips? In short, no. That's because in Italian *ravioli* means exactly what it means in English: mini stuffed pasta parcels. Purists may point out that *ravioli* came to denote pasta with a vegetable or vegetable-and-cheese filling from the area of Liguria specifically (as distinct from tortellini and other kinds of stuffed pasta), but whatever the finer points of filling types and regions, the word certainly doesn't mean 'little turnips', despite what various cookery books and websites might tell you. To put it another way: in English, the phrase 'hot dog' literally means 'a dim-witted hairy animal of a high temperature', but if you order one in a café you'll get a tube of stinky processed offal in a soggy bread roll; by contrast, in Italian, *ravioli* doesn't have a literal meaning of 'little turnips' – it only has the pasta sense.

It is just possible that the term derives from a dialect word meaning 'little turnip' (*rapa* is Italian for 'turnip'), perhaps relating to the shape of the pasta parcels, while another theory is that it derives from a Genoese dialect word for 'bits and pieces' or 'leftovers', reflecting the variable types of filling; but no one is really sure about the origin of the Italian word *ravioli*. It might also be related to the verb *ravvolgere*, 'to wrap up', but any concrete proof has been lost in the mists of time: the first Italian and English recipes for ravioli date from the thirteenth and fourteenth centuries, with numerous spellings used in the two languages, such as 'rauiole', 'raphiole', 'rabiole' and 'rabiola'.

## VERDICT: FALSE

If it's any consolation, no one knows for definite when or why the English phrase 'hot dog' was coined, either.

# There's only one train station in Singapore

AS SINGAPORE IS AN ISLAND, this is potentially very bad news for anyone wanting to take a day trip by rail, unless the authorities have constructed a scenic circular route around the island. Fortunately, however, this claim is total rubbish, so no such problem exists.

First, there's the small matter of the MRT, the Mass Rapid Transit system, which is blatantly a railway. The first section of the MRT opened to passengers in 1987, and even back then no one thought 'Let's open the first station before the second one is ready, just so we can say we've got a train station'. Today there are over 60 MRT stations across the country, connected by around 100 km (62 miles) of standard-gauge track. In addition there is also the LRT, or Light Rapid Transit system, which is like a collection of three miniature MRTs, each network linking together large housing developments, and connecting with the MRT itself. There are currently 31 operational LRT stations, although in the spirit of forward planning, some 14 additional

stations have been constructed but not opened yet – they're waiting for someone to build some housing in the area first.

Perhaps those who want to stick to their guns will complain that the LRT and MRT stops aren't 'proper' train stations, because rapid-transit and light-rail systems, which only transport people and not freight, aren't 'full-blown' railways. For example, the North East MRT Line is entirely underground and is a totally driverless, computer-controlled system, which perhaps means to train purists that it doesn't connect 'train stations'. This would be unnecessarily harsh. However, other locations that really *would* be tenuous candidates for 'train stations' are the terminal stops of the Changi Airport Skytrain, and the stations on Singapore's two monorail systems: the Sentosa Express (which has four stations, of which three are currently operational, connecting Singapore's main island with the small resort island of Sentosa) and the Panorail at Jurong Bird Park (which boasts three stations, and the intriguing distinction of being the only monorail in the world to pass 'inside a walk-in aviary').

In fact Singapore could happily get away with just a single 'real' train station, since it's linked to the Malay peninsula by the Johor–Singapore causeway, which carries road traffic and a railway line from Woodlands in Singapore across the Straits of Johor to Johor Bahru in Malaysia. (The Malaysia–Singapore Second Link, or Tuas Second Link, which opened in 1998 and links Tanjung Kupang in Johor with Tuas in Singapore, only carries road traffic.) Even within Singapore, however, there are two train stations on the railway line to Malaysia where passengers can alight: the terminus, at Tanjong Pagar (also known as Keppel Road) in downtown Singapore, and the Woodlands Train Checkpoint in the north, which is where Singaporean authorities carry out passport and customs checks. Technically, however, the Tanjong Pagar station premises – and all the track from there to Woodlands, including a loop station at Bukit Timah in central Singapore where passengers can't currently get on or off – belongs to the Malaysian rail operator Keretapi Tanah Melayu, under the terms of a 999-year lease.

So perhaps the garbled origin of the 'only one station' idea is connected to the fact that the railway doesn't even belong to Singapore. But it's probably more likely to be an out-of-date claim originating before the Woodlands Train Checkpoint opened, and possibly even before the MRT was built. Either way, in today's Singapore, there is *definitely* more than one train station.

## VERDICT: FALSE

Due to a tedious dispute between the two countries, Malaysia carries out its passport and customs checks for passengers leaving Singapore at the southern terminus of Tanjong Pagar, meaning that travellers are granted entry to Malaysia before they have left Singapore and before they have even had their passports checked by the Singaporean authorities on the way out.

# The Greek national anthem has 158 verses

MOST PEOPLE HAVE DIFFICULTY remembering anything beyond the first verse of a national anthem, and it's always entertaining to watch professional footballers pretending to mouth some vague approximation of their national anthem at the start of a match. But asking anyone to remember 158 verses – let alone remain patriotically standing for that time – really is a bit of a stretch. It would be about as appealing as sitting through the whole of the movie *Bicentennial Man*.

Thankfully for Greek citizens, the official national anthem only consists of two verses, and does not involve Robin Williams pretending to be a loveable robot. However, the reason the song is often claimed to be so much longer is that the words of the official anthem are the first two stanzas of an epic poem written in 1823 by Dionysios Solomos, known in English as 'Hymn to Freedom' or 'Hymn to Liberty', set to music by Nikolaos Mantzaros. The poem does consist of 158 stanzas, the first 24 of which were adopted as the country's anthem in 1865, although it was later decided that just the first two were more than enough, thank you very much. In some sort of bulk-buy arrangement, Cyprus also uses the same two-verse anthem.

The poem itself specifically celebrates the Greek War of Independence of the 1820s, following which Greece separated from the Ottoman Empire, although the first two verses just represent some general waffle about liberty and swords and stuff.

## VERDICT: FALSE

A much more interesting-sounding national anthem is that of the Russian republic of Tuva, 'Tooruktug Dolgaï Tangdym', which translates as 'The Forest is Full of Pine Nuts', and is an aspirational song about getting rich from rearing livestock.

# The longest corridor in the world is in the Falkland Islands

THE FALKLAND ISLANDS (or the Malvinas, depending whose side you're on) aren't very big. Consisting of the two main islands – East Falkland and West Falkland – and around 200 much smaller islands, the total land area is a little over 12,000 square kilometres (around 4,700 square miles), so to the man in the pub it seems amusing that the world's longest corridor should be situated there. You'd think it might be in a secret military base somewhere underneath Nevada, which the US government aren't telling us about; or on board Darth Vader's Death Star, if the Death Star wasn't just the fictional creation of a film director who was told to grow a beard by Francis Ford Coppola.

You may be pleased to learn that the truth contains elements of both these scenarios. The longest corridor in the world, approximately 1 mile (1,610 metres) in length, is at the Mount Pleasant Royal Air Force base on East Falkland – and used to be nicknamed 'the Death Star corridor' until a bunch of art students from Scotland's Dundee University were invited to work with the base's military personnel to redesign, redecorate and 'humanise' the formerly drab corridor. When the project was completed in 1999 the passageway, with its new 'art stations', became known as the Millennium Corridor – on the basis that anything anyone did in 1999 had to have the word 'millennium' attached to it, preferably misspelt as 'millenium'.

There is a fair bit of competition around. For example, the Long Corridor at Beijing's Summer Palace is impressively long, but at 728 metres (2,388 feet) it's considerably shorter than the Millennium Corridor; and it's an outdoor covered walkway, so it doesn't really count anyway. The pillared corridors at the Ramanathaswamy Temple in Rameswaram, India, have a total length of around 1,200 metres (3,900 feet), though the longest single stretch is about 210 metres (around 690 feet). When north London's Colney Hatch Asylum was built in the 1800s, it claimed to feature the longest corridor in Europe, and some said the world, at around 240 metres (790 feet), but when the hospital was redeveloped as luxury housing during the 1990s, the single unbroken corridor was eliminated. Another English hospital with an impressive corridor length is St James's in Leeds, where a ring corridor around the site stretches to 946 metres (3,100 feet), although this is categorised by the hospital as being 40 per cent public corridor and 60 per cent service walkways. The optimistically named Infinite Corridor at the Massachusetts Institute of Technology turns out to be a mere 251 metres (825 feet).

Another possibility might be the collection of pedestrian tunnels underneath downtown Houston, which have a total length of around 10 km (6 miles) – but do they, or other similar networks of foot tunnels, even count as corridors? Disappointingly, the International Organization for Standardization hasn't laid down specific guidelines for distinguishing an underground corridor from a simple tunnel – although ISO 6707-1:2004 defines a corridor as 'a narrow enclosed circulation space that gives access to rooms or other spaces'. So with doors leading to rooms, not having direct access to the open air, and being a single continuous walkway, the Millennium Corridor holds on to its position as the longest corridor in the world.

### VERDICT: TRUE

The abbreviation by which the International Organization for Standardization is known, ISO, doesn't stand for anything: they decided that because abbreviations in different languages would vary, it was better to practise what they preach and use a standard abbreviation, which derives from the Greek word *isos*, meaning 'equal'. Smart-arses.

# ACKNOWLEDGEMENTS

I am most grateful to my skilled and patient editor, Sarah Lavelle, whose experience and guidance ensured that my raw materials were fashioned into an excellent finished article. My thanks also go to the rest of the team at Ebury, including Vicky Orchard and Caroline Newbury. As with *Bears Can't Run Downhill*, the fantastic design is due to the efforts of Nicky Barneby, Tony Lyons and Two Associates, while Sarah Nayler, via NB Illustration, once again crafted the visual treats that add so much to the book's appeal. James Sleigh provided many a contribution for illustration ideas, Lisa Footitt created the comprehensive index and Vicki Vrint carried out the precision proof-reading. I would also like to thank Kate Pool and the Society of Authors for their assistance in professional matters.

Many thanks to those who responded to my odd requests for information and who helped me get my facts straight, as well as those who helped out directly or indirectly with various comments and suggestions – even if I didn't always make use of those suggestions due to constraints of time, space or my own stupidity: Ian Aspinall; Australia Zoo; Chris Ball (I never did eat all those cabbages); Hankey Bannister; Carl Bird (West Midlands Police); Justine Bird; Joe Chesterman-March; Mick Faver; Marty(n) Gabel;

Andrew Gay; Louise Gollan (Lothian & Borders Police); Dick Harlow (Police National Legal Database, UK); Deborah Heath; Pam Inglis; Adv. Johan Jonck (ArriveAlive); Nicky Jones; Gavin Kelly (Department of Transport, South Africa); Nick Kouppari; Land Transport New Zealand; Dominique Lazanski; Núria López Mercader; Bob Millard (Driving Standards Agency, UK); Michala Meades (even though I didn't use your 'barmy' fact); Grace J. Nielsen (Nuuk Tourism); Tim Nielsen and Emma Yengi (Adelaide Zoo); Pam Parton; Corine Phipps (Greater Manchester Police); Lucy Reid; Ron Richards; Patrick Rodger; Tim Rodger; Haydn Smith; Pamela Smith (Perth Zoo); Dr Neal Spencer (The British Museum); Dimitra Stafilia; Alan Thawley; Peter Trait (formerly trading as Simon Turner); Su Turner (St James's University Hospital, Leeds); Shelley Waldon (Melbourne Zoo); Alex Ward; Emma Ward; Nerys Wilkinson; Jim Williams (New South Wales Police); Mark Williams (Taronga Zoo); Margaret Winn (Woolsthorpe Manor); and Brenda Zanin (Royal Canadian Mounted Police).

In addition I would like to extend my gratitude to the many people who helped make *Bears Can't Run Downhill* a success once it hit the shops, boosted by the relentless promotional efforts of the Barry, Jeger and Timms families. In particular I'd like to thank Ben Prater of BBC Radio Bristol, along with Sacha Bigwood and the rest of the Drivetime team, for allowing me to waffle on about shattering tarantulas, poisonous nutmeg and biro-sized mice over a number of months.

Last of all, but most importantly, my biggest thanks are due to Karen Jeger for her patience and assistance, and I hereby officially put into print my promise to buy us a dishwasher.

# INDEX